Gypsy Violins

By Steve Piskor

Hungarian/Slovak Gypsies in America

Visit Gypsyviolins.com
MySpace.com/gypsyviolins
Facebook.com/gypsyviolins
Twitter.com/gypsyviolins

Published by
Saroma™
1215 w.10th Suite 709
Cleveland, Ohio 44113

Library of Congress Control Number: 2012903498

ISBN 978-0-578099-897

This book is dedicated to all of our ancestors who had
the courage to endure
the hardship of moving to this country, to have the
strength to survive discrimination
and humiliation, to have the will
to keep going, and to make life better for us.
I thank you.
Your efforts are appreciated, and they will never be forgotten.

I also dedicate this book to my father and mother:
Julius Piskor born 1930 died 1986
and Esther (Mitzi) née Ballog born 1933.

And to all my nieces and nephews: Angel, George, Gavin,
Logan, Tisha, Dominic, Aliyah, Vicky, Jenel, Victor, Tabitha,
James, Vincent, Mia, Natalya, Vito Jr., Donny, Evan, Jenny,
Stephanie, Jonathon, Aubriella, Kevin, Justin, Jill, Peter,
Mike, and Kelly.

CONTENTS

Introduction

This book offers a rare look at the Hungarian/Slovak Gypsies who have been in this country for over 120 years. This is the first book ever written about these Gypsies. Many books, publications, journals, and newspaper articles mention these Gypsies, but none of the pieces were connected. This book puts the documented history together to tell the story of this particular group of Gypsies. They were all fine musicians, playing in many of the best places around America for over one hundred years. They have made their mark in history. They have played for presidents, dignitaries, and special events throughout the country. This group numbers a few thousand people who are either related or know one other. If you have ever heard Gypsy musicians play, then you have heard these people play.

They brought the traditional Gypsy music they and their ancestors had played in Europe for hundreds of years. They are directly linked to Europe's finest Hungarian Gypsy musicians. They never told fortunes, traveled in caravans, or performed in a circus. Today the traditional Gypsy orchestra is gone, with only a handful of musicians still playing. They have lost their heritage, and Gypsies under the age of fifty don't even know it. The Gypsy funeral has been recorded in newspapers and books for over one hundred years in America; today it is gone. Everyone asks, "What happened to the Gypsy violins, orchestras, and funerals?" This book traces their history from the time they came to America, answers the question of what happened to them, and shows the gradual loss of the Gypsy heritage.

bevezetés

Ez a könyv kínál egy ritka pillantást a magyar / szlovák cigányok, akik ebben az országban több mint 120 éve. Ez az első könyv, amit valaha is írtak ezekről a cigányok. Sok könyvek, kiadványok, folyóiratok és újságcikkek említi a cigányok, de egyik darabja volt kapcsolatos. Ez a könyv hozza a dokumentált történelem együtt mesélik el e különleges csoportjának cigányok. Mindannyian jó zenész, játszik számos, a legjobb helyek körül Amerikában több mint száz éve. Ők tették a jelet a történelemben. Ők játszottak az elnökök, méltóságok, és a különleges események egész országban. Ez a csoport számokat, néhány ezer ember, akik vagy tudják kapcsolatos, vagy egy másik. Ha valaha is hallott cigány zenészek játszanak, akkor hallottam ezeket az embereket játszani.

Ők hozták magukkal a hagyományos cigány zenét ők és elődeik játszott Európában több száz éve. Ezek közvetlenül Európa legjobb magyar cigányzenészek. Soha nem jósoltak, utazott lakókocsik, vagy elvégzett egy cirkusz. Ma a hagyományos cigány zenekar eltűnt, csak néhány zenész is játszik. Ők elvesztették örökséget, és cigányok év alatti 50 nem is tud róla. A cigány temetés rögzítésre került újságok és könyvek több mint száz éve Amerikában, ma is elment. Mindenki azt kérdezi: "Mi történt a cigány hegedű, zenekarok és temetéseken?" Ez a könyv végigköveti a történelem az időben jöttek Amerikába, választ ad arra a kérdésre, hogy mi történt velük, és megmutatja a fokozatos elvesztése a cigány örökség.

Úvod

Táto kniha ponúka unikátny pohľad na maďarskej / slovenský Rómov, ktorí boli v tejto krajine viac ako 120 rokov. Je to prvá kniha, aká kedy bola napísaná o týchto Cigánov. Veľa kníh, publikácií, časopisov a novinových článkov uviesť tieto cigánov, ale žiadna zo skladieb boli pripojené. Táto kniha stavia zdokumentovanú históriu spoločne rozprávať príbeh tejto skupiny Rómov. Všetci boli jemné hudobníci, hrať v mnohých z najlepších miest na celom Amerike pre viac ako sto rokov. Oni urobili ich znamenie v histórii. Oni hrali pre prezidentmi, hodnostárov a špeciálnych akcií po celej krajine. Táto skupina čísel niekoľko tisíc ľudí, ktorí sú buď súvisiace alebo viete, jeden ďalší týždeň Ak ste niekedy počuli cigánskej hudobníci hrajú, a potom ste počul títo ľudia hrajú.

Oni priniesli tradičnú cigánsku hudbu oni a ich predkovia hrali v Európe po staročia. Sú priamo spojené s najlepšími európskymi maďarských rómskych hudobníkov. Oni nikdy nepovedal bohatstvo, cestoval v karavanoch, alebo hral v cirkuse. Dnes tradičné cigánsky orchester je preč, len s niekoľkými hudobníkmi stále hrajú. Stratili svoje dedičstvo, a Cigáni do veku päťdesiatich ani vedieť. Gypsy pohreb bol zaznamenaný v novinách a knihách viac ako sto rokov v Amerike, dnes je to preč. Každý sa pýta: "Čo sa stalo s cigánskych huslí, orchestre a pohreby?" Táto kniha mapuje ich históriu od doby, kedy prišiel do Ameriky, odpovedá na otázku, čo sa im stalo, a ukazuje na postupnú stratu rómskej dedičstva.

ABOUT THE AUTHOR

I, Steve Piskor, was born in Cleveland, Ohio, in 1954. I graduated high school in 1973 and studied law for two years to become a paralegal. I also attended Cuyahoga Community College. I studied guitar when I was young, but by the time I was thirteen, I went to work. Between work and school, I had to put learning guitar on hold.

As far back as I can remember, I have been interested in Gypsies. At twelve years old, I was going to hear the men play; by fifteen, I was taking pictures and movies of funerals. In my teens, I started researching Gypsies in general. I wanted to see where they came from, whether they had a flag, why there were so many different types of Gypsies. To my surprise, I found out that the Cleveland Public Library has one of the largest collections of Gypsy material in the world. They have hundreds of books about Gypsies. There were no computers back then, but the library had an index on these books, so that was a good place to start. After I read a few books, a librarian noticed the subject I was researching and showed me the books from the Gypsy Lore Society. The books were set in volumes, like a set of encyclopedias, dating back to the late nineteenth century; each volume has two hundred to three hundred pages, and there are about twenty volumes.

The Cleveland Public Library has one of the few complete sets in the country. To my amazement, when I started my research, I began finding material specific to the Gypsies who were from Cleveland and Braddock. This sparked my appetite for more, and my research went in a new direction. I began searching for these people I had read about. These Gypsies refer to each other as cousins, whether they are related or not.

In 1980 I joined the Gypsy Lore Society. The group was located in England at that time, but then moved their headquarters to the United States in 1988. In the 1990s I began genealogical research and joined the Western Reserve Historical Society, which was one of the largest in the country. For the last twenty years, I have documented everything I found about these Gypsies. I have done research in Cleveland, Pittsburgh, Braddock, Youngstown, Detroit, and Chicago. I purchased a computer over twenty years ago; there was no Internet then, but you could access some databases such as the Cleveland Public Library, which only showed their listing. Since then I have done much online research and was among the first in line to access Ellis Island. I have many birth, death, marriage, census, immigration, and cemetery records of Gypsies. I am continuing with my genealogical studies and plan to further my studies in Kassa, Hungary, which today is Kosice, Slovakia.

Steve Piskor

Are we Gypsy or Roma

The word Roma and Romani have been used in English since the 19th century as an alternative for Gypsy. Today Romani Rights Organizations are fighting to change the term "Gypsy" to "Roma". They feel Gypsy has been used as a stereotype in a negative way to describe this race of people. When gadje (non-Gypsies) think of the word Gypsy the associate them as thieves, con artist, baby stealers, travelers in covered wagons, low life, dirty, uneducated, worthless, fortune tellers, witches, evil…and there's more, but I'm sure you get the idea. Today Gypsy-Roma websites use the term Roma, now all of their articles about the discrimination against Gypsies say discrimination against Roma. Now we have another term Gadje can use the same way they use the term Gypsy. The term Gypsy is not what is being discriminated against; it's the people that are subjected to the atrocities committed against them worldwide. We still have discrimination and stereotyping, now with a term that didn't work in the past. Many countries use the term Gypsy, the Spanish term is Gitano, the French term is Gitan, and both derived from the word Gypsy. In Romania the Romany-Gypsy people have asked Parliament in in Bucharest to accept a proposal to change the official name of the Romany from Roma to Tigan. The term Cigan – Cigany or a variation of the spelling is used throughout Europe. Today Romani Rights Activist needs to promote Spain's tolerance of Gypsies, which is a "Model" for what should happen in the rest of the world. In Spain Roma say they are first Spanish, then Gypsy, and they are proud to be both. In Spain's almost one million Gypsies five percent of Gypsies live in make shift camps, half of Roma are homeowners, almost all have healthcare, and at least seventy five percent have some sort of steady income. The country spends thirty six million dollars annually for Gypsies. Today in Hungary there is much discrimination against Roma-Gypsies. Livia Jaroka is the first Roma member of the European Parliament. Livia Jaroka is the great niece of the great Gypsy violinist Sandor Jaroka. In January of 2012, Livia Jaroka said she was shocked the way some of her colleagues used the situation of Roma in a manipulating way stating that Roma live in fear in Hungary. She said, **I firmly reject such false allegations and I would like to remind everyone that the current Hungarian government has taken more steps for the equal opportunities of Roma than most governments in the past 20 years.** I talked with two Romani-Gypsy Rights Activist; one said I wish you would have changed the name of the book to "Roma Violins", which in my opinion would do no justice to the book or the Gypsies that the book is written about. The second said my book has too much "Gypsyness" in the book and asked if there was any attempt to educate the general culture about the real Roma or Romani culture. He says I have not read the book yet or any of its content. When you talk about Gypsy discrimination, this is the worst discrimination a Gypsy can get. In other words Hungarian-Slovak Gypsies are not real Gypsies because they are not called Roma. I think this guy is watching too much TV and movies and should not use Roma or Gypsy to further his own personal gain. I have had to hide my race my entire life and I will not hide behind the term Roma. This book is written about 100% Gypsies when they were Gypsies. Today the Gypsy Lore Society has not changed their name to the Roma Lore Society, the Gypsy Kings have not changed their name to the Roma Kings, the Budapest 100 Piece Gypsy Orchestra have not changed their name to the Budapest 100 Piece Roma Orchestra, and there are so many more I could write another book about it. The use of the term "Gypsy" is what we are and instead of focusing all your attention on the change of the name, you should put your efforts in to helping Roma-Gypsies. I would also like to state that not all Roma-Gypsy activists are like this, some are actually doing a great job and without their efforts Roma-Gypsies would have no one else to speak for them. The term "Gypsy is not discriminating or stereotypical if used in the proper sense. This book does not use the word "Gypsy" in a negative way. People that see the word "Gypsy" in a demeaning way are the ones that need to be educated.

Gypsy or Roma
(for the Roma activist)

The word "Gypsy" is a discriminating word that the Romani Rights Organization is trying to change to Roma. The word Gypsy is compared to the "N" word that has been erased from use throughout the world. We hope to do the same with the "G" word. I used Gypsy in the book because most people are unaware of the word "Roma". We have to continue to correct people on the use of the proper word. The use of the word "Gypsy" is so stereotypically wrong that the TV series "My Big Fat Gypsy Wedding" used the word to associate these Gadje as Gypsies because their behavior is what is expected of the use of the word Gypsy. In America the word "Gypsy" is commonly used as a reference to a lifestyle or fashion, and not to the Romani ethnicity. Roma throughout the world have had to deny their ethnicity and change their names to Italian sounding names, Hungarian-Slovak Roma have to say they are Hungarian or Slovak and hide the Roma because of worldwide discrimination when the word Gypsy is used. Help erase the word "Gypsy" and only use the word "Roma"

Slovakia as it is today.

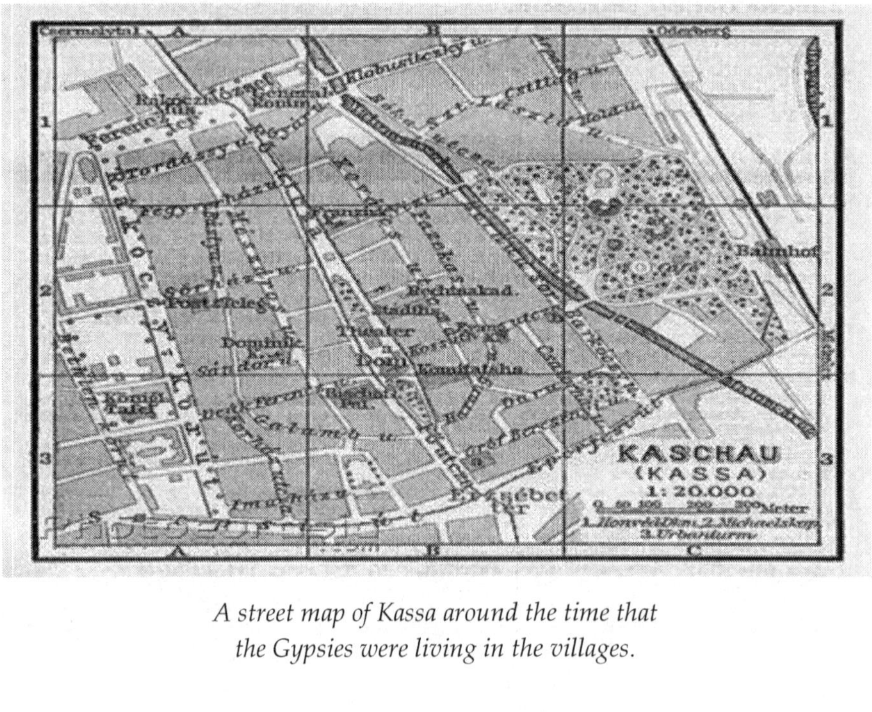

A street map of Kassa around the time that the Gypsies were living in the villages.

BRADDOCK

In the mid-1880s, the first of the Gypsies arrived in the United States, coming from the villages of Kassa, Hungary, known today as Kosice, Slovakia. During most of its existence, Kosice (Kassa) was part of Hungary; it came under Czechoslovakian rule in 1920. In 1993, after the breakup of Czechoslovakia, Kosice became part of an independent Slovakia. These early Gypsy pioneers left Hungary under the rule of Franz Joseph and settled in Cleveland, Ohio; Braddock, Pennsylvania; and Youngstown, Ohio.

This was not an easy trip to make, and the decision to make it involved the whole family and sometimes the whole village. It took a long time to save money and plan. The Gypsies had to obtain permission from Hungary to leave, and after 1900 a passport was needed. Ellis Island opened in 1892.

Most of the Gypsies came one at a time or in pairs, usually an adult and child. Some children made the arduous journey over with a friend or relative. The men came first so they could make money to send for the rest of the family.

The average steerage ticket on a ship cost thirty U.S. dollars, which included a bed and meals. In the poor villages of Kassa, thirty dollars was well over two months pay, but many families

Kassa, Hungary, circa 1900, around the same time some of the Gypsies were still living in the villages, getting ready to immigrate to the United States.

Many would travel the 744 miles to the port of Bremen, Germany, by train. When they arrived at the port of departure, were willing to scrape by, save, and go without to afford the passage to America they often had to wait days and sometimes even months for paperwork or for the ship to arrive. Then, before they were allowed to board the ship, they had to answer questions, be examined by a doctor, and receive the required vaccinations.

Once on board the ship, they were taken down long, cramped stairwells to the lower decks of the ship, where they remained for the entire voyage. Some of the larger ships held between 1500 and 2000 steerage passengers. Deck visits were limited, the food was horrible, and bunk beds were stacked on top of each other. The smell was horrific and conditions were terrible. Many passengers did not survive the voyage, which could last from ten days to a month depending on weather conditions and the ship.

Once they arrived at the port in the United States, they were subjected to the same process they completed at their port of departure: they saw a doctor, answered questions, and waited for more paperwork. Fortunately, the immigration officials spoke several languages and did not change the names of the Gypsies to more Americanized names, they worked off the paperwork from the point of departure. Those that did not meet the health, mental, and legal requirements to enter the U.S. were sent back. Children twelve years old and up were sent back alone; those under twelve had to have a parent or guardian accompany them on the long journey home.

After they were admitted into the United States, they had to travel 461 miles to Cleveland, 400 miles to Youngstown, and 350 miles to Braddock. One of the questions on the ship's manifest was, "How much money do you have, or do you have more than $30?" Most immigrants had less than ten dollars in their pocket when they arrived. After World War I immigration laws changed and limits were set on how many immigrants could enter America.

****

In 1875 Andrew Carnegie opened his first steel plant, the Edgar Thomson Works, in Braddock, Pennsylvania. In 1883 Andrew Carnegie purchased the Homestead Steel Works, a rival mill. In just a few years, Carnegie became a very wealthy man; the demand for steel was so great there was a back order for steel. By 1901 Andrew Carnegie had sold the plant to J. P. Morgan for $480 million, equivalent to about $120 billion today, which made him one of the richest men in the world and contributed to the birth of U.S. Steel.

The steel mills were an important part of the migration of not only the Gypsies but of all immigrants because they created jobs. Thousands of Hungarians and Slovaks and many other ethnic people from Europe immigrated to the Pittsburgh area. While the steel mills were employing thousands of workers, the towns of Braddock, Homestead, and Pittsburgh flourished.

Braddock, Pennsylvania, Gypsies circa 1920s.

Braddock's population in 1900 was 15,654. Braddock Avenue had many stores like Saks Fifth Avenue, movie theaters, restaurants, grocery stores, and much more. The Gypsies didn't have to go far. Andrew Carnegie built has first steel mill, the Edgar Thomas Works, and the first Carnegie Library in the country in Braddock, Pennsylvania.

There was a growing demand for more stores, pharmacies, grocers, restaurants, taverns, and entertainment. These Gypsies knew this, and that's one of the main reasons why they settled in Braddock and Homestead, Pennsylvania.

These Gypsies were Hungarian and Slovak musicians, the third largest community of Roma in the United States. They spoke the Gypsy (Romany) dialect, which had its start from the ancient Sanskrit language of India. They were also known as Bashadle Gypsies and sometimes grouped together with the Gypsies of Romania as Boyash Gypsies. In Hungary they are called "Romange" Roma which means Hungarian Gypsy. They also spoke Slovak and Hungarian. They came to the United States playing Gypsy music of the Old World. All of these Gypsies that came to America were very fine musicians. Many of them went on to play in the Pittsburgh, Cleveland, Chicago, Detroit, and Baltimore Symphonies. Many became well-known throughout America, making many records, TV appearances, and radio broadcasts, and they were mentioned in newspaper stories.

These Gypsies were descendants of the musicians who played with famous Gypsy orchestras such as Janos Bihari (1764–1827), whose descendants today are the Lakatos family: female Gypsy violinist Czinka Panna (d. 1772), Pista Danko (1848–1903), Jansci Rigo, Imre Magyari, and Racz Laci. They were descendants of the same Gypsies who influenced such composers as Joseph Haydn; Franz Liszt, who wrote fifteen Hungarian rhapsodies; Johannes Brahms, who wrote twenty-one Hungarian dances; Antonín Dvořák; Pablo de Sarasate, who wrote *Zigeunerweisen*; George Bizet, who wrote *Carmen*; Maurice Ravel; and many more.

Braddock, Pennsylvania Gypsies
Photo courtesy of Tony Selepsky.

This is probably a good time to say that these Hungarian/Slovak Gypsies were not stereotypical Gypsies. They never told fortunes or traveled in caravans. They respected the law and blended into society unnoticed—until they played their music. They took great pride in the ability to play music, and they were proud to be Gypsy. They lived by their music and died by their music, as they had for hundreds of years.

All of these Gypsies immigrated to the United States between 1885 and 1910. Braddock, Homestead, Uniontown and Johnstown Pennsylvania, Cleveland and Youngstown, Ohio, Gary, Indiana, and New York City all had Gypsies from this group. A few thousand Gypsies came from four to five hundred families. In Braddock, the Gypsies lived by 10th Street, between Braddock Avenue and Talbot Avenue. Throughout the years the Gypsies lived in two courtyards. The first yard was closer to Braddock Avenue and 10th Street between Pine Way and Braddock Avenues. They lived in this courtyard for over thirty years. It was described as row houses, built so they all shared a courtyard. The Gypsies called it the "Braddock yard."

A book written in the 1920s states, "Some two hundred Hungarian Gypsies, for instance, have purchased a solid block

Photo Courtesy of William Ballog.
This picture is of the first Braddock yard, circa 1930s.
The name of the courtyard was "Hands Court."
Braddock Gypsies on the porch, among them is Fannie (Funna) Hallup.

Hands Court "Braddock Yard."
Photo Courtesy of Tony Selepsky.

in a Pennsylvania city, where they have lived for years." A Gypsy by the name of Vongood Pohlatko (Polo) purchased these houses. (I will try to spell Gypsy names as they sound). He purchased these homes so the Gypsies in the community of Braddock were settled. In a 1920s publication by the Gypsy Lore Society an article states, "The Gypsies in the borough of Braddock, PA, have purchased an entire block of homes, making them the largest community of settled Gypsies in the United States."

When these Gypsies were in Kassa, Hungary, they lived in small villages. The whole village was related in one way or another or through marriage. The same held true of the Gypsies who lived in other villages. History shows that they lived this way for hundreds of years in Kassa, Hungary, so that when they arrived in the United States, coming from a country that was not friendly to Gypsies, they didn't know what to expect in the U.S. Their instinct was to stick together; the same way that they had survived in Kassa. In Braddock's Hands Court, the homes were purchased so they could live next door to each other, and no one could throw them out. In Cleveland on West 24th Street and Columbus Road, they lived next door to each other. In Homestead they lived within walking distance to one another. In Detroit's Delray district and in Chicago on Burling Avenue, they lived next door to each other.

In Youngstown on Boardman Street, they lived next door to each other. The same was true for Gary, Indiana, Johnstown, Uniontown, and New York City. This was security for them. They watched over, respected, and helped each other. They had a strong family bond that had run deep for hundreds of years. In the United States, they continued to live this way for over eighty years. "United We Stand, Divided We Fall." I guess we all learned that lesson.

Today these Gypsies number in the few thousand. I went to a wedding in Chicago, and there were over six hundred Gypsies at the reception; I didn't know five hundred of them. Because these Gypsies lived together for hundreds of years, I could find out who anyone was at the reception by asking them who their parents were or who the grandparents or great-grandparents were, and I would know who the family was, what city they were from, and how they were related.

Throughout the years, many reporters, authors, and historians visited the Gypsies of Braddock. In another book from the 1920s (*Gypsy Fires in America*, 1924, p. 214), the author, Irving Brown, tells a story about traveling through Pittsburgh when the train stopped in Braddock. He remembered that a large community of Gypsies lived there. When he found them a short distance away, he told them he was writing a book and wanted to interview them. They welcomed him in.

A group of Gypsy children in the Braddock yard, circa mid 1940s.
My mother Mitzi (Ballog) Piskor is kneeling in front.

In this picture you can get an idea of how the houses were set up with the corner in the shape of an L.
Photo courtesy of Tony Selepsky

The second Braddock yard is in the background of this Gypsy Funeral picture. This view is from Talbot and 10th Streets, in the alley.
Photos are property of the author.

Gypsy musicians march in a funeral procession down Braddock Avenue, circa 1930.

Brown said forty to fifty families lived in houses that formed a rough square. The Gypsy men quickly formed an orchestra with two cimbaloms back to back and began to play. The women spread out a table with food and drink for everyone. By nightfall, and after a few glasses of wine, the musicians were still playing, now with more madness to their czardas and more emotion to their slow songs. I would guess it cost this author a few gallons of wine, but what a cheap price to pay for such an experience. On the same page he also mentioned the Countess Verona from Cleveland.

I could only imagine what that orchestra must have sounded like. With the Gypsies living next door to each other and musicians in every house, there was music in the yard every day, about one hundred musicians practicing, teaching, and rehearsing as an orchestra. It was pretty easy to put together an orchestra at a moment's notice at that time.

A Gypsies' life is about music, and he or she starts learning an instrument at an early age, between five and ten years old.

Four year old Randy Margitza already playing with the Gypsy Orchestra

Gypsy kids practicing in the Braddock Yard

The instruments are handed down. If the father played the bass, he would teach his son the bass. In some families the father, grandfather, uncles, and brothers all played the same instrument. Most of the Gypsies wanted their sons to play violin and become a Primas (lead violinist).

Most Gypsies could play multiple instruments, even at an early age. If the child wanted to play another instrument, the family would encourage him or her to try another one to see where his or her talent was. Many of the children started out on piano because it gave them a good foundation to learn music, then they moved on to the instrument of their choice. Many of these Gypsies had to play multiple musical instruments to survive.

There were many teachers in the Gypsy communities. While some children took lessons from professional teachers and learned how to read music, most of them learned how to play by ear. The only difference between the two was the ability to read music. Famous concert violinist Itzhak Perlman said, "I wish I had that wonderful Gypsy tone." Reading music is important, but you also need to have the talent to play.

A visitor in New York was looking for Carnegie Hall when he saw a man walking, holding a violin case. He stopped the man and asked, "Sir, how do you get to Carnegie Hall?" And the man replied, "Practice, lots of practice." While this joke is funny, it also has meaning. The Gypsy children practiced for hours a day. I can remember parents coming out of their houses, looking for their kids who had to go home to practice. Fathers would sit with the child and play along with their lesson until the child learned it. In the Braddock yard, it was a common sight to see a group of musicians practicing. In the public schools, the music teachers loved the Gypsy kids.

A Gypsy funeral at the Braddock Catholic Cemetery. Photos are property of the author.

Circa 1940's. Pohlatko (Polo) funeral.

A Gypsy stopped a newspaper cameraman who was sent out to Braddock to take photos for an article published in the Pittsburgh Press 1948. "You can't take any pictures around here unless you see the old lady," someone told him.

"Do you mean the queen?" he asked.

"Naw," was the reply.

"Oh, the princess?" he asked.

"Naw, I mean the old lady. She has the say around here."

"Is she a member of your tribe?" the reporter asked.

"Naw," said the Gypsy again. "She's Irish. I'm talking about the landlady."

There were no kings, queens, or other royalty among these Gypsies, just a lot of great musicians.

In the late 1930s, the first Braddock yard was sold to a developer who built a warehouse on the site. The Gypsies made the short move from 10th Street and Braddock Avenue to 10th Street and Talbot Avenue to the second Braddock yard, between Talbot Avenue and Pine Way. The second yard was similar to the first one. The row houses formed a square yard that all of the families shared, with gangways in the front and back for access to the yard. This group of Gypsies lived in this yard until the early 1960s. All of the Gypsies from Braddock eventually moved to the Detroit, Michigan, area.

I have found at least fifteen books, journals, and publications (not including many newspaper articles) that mentioned the Gypsies of Braddock. In two publications from the Gypsy Lore Society, they interviewed Julia Margitza. She talked about her famous sister, Verona Miko.

In another publication they interviewed Jerry Lacy, and he told them he was a musician, a bass player. The Gypsy Lore Society started in 1888 in England, and then they moved their

Braddock Funerals 1930s
Photographs courtesy of Tony Selepsky

headquarters to the United States in 1989. They produce a publication, and I have shared many of their articles about the Hungarian Gypsies in this book. On their website they describe the Hungarian/Slovak Gypsies as: mainly sedentary Gypsies found primarily in the industrial cities of the northern U.S.; they number in the few thousand and are noted for playing "Gypsy music" in cafés, night clubs, and restaurants.

Other publications that include information on the Gypsies of Braddock are: *The Subject of Index to Periodicals* Volume 1915; *The Survey* by the Charity Organization Society of the City of New York, Survey Associates; a German publication titled *Bibliographies de Musikschriftums,* 1936; *The Canadian Journal of Economics and Political Science*; and *The Encyclopedia Britannica,* 1956. There were many authors, journalists, researchers, anthropologists, students, and the curious who went to Braddock to see these Gypsies. Most people were studying Gypsies in general. They found that the Hungarian/Slovak Gypsies were different from other Gypsies in America in that they were very much opposed to the lifestyle of the traveling Gypsies.

The Braddock Gypsy community welcomed the chance to let people know they were different; they didn't fit the stereotype that most people knew. An article in a newspaper in 1899 reported that two doctors failed to disclose one case of diphtheria found in Braddock, which ended in a fatality. The two doctors were charged for not reporting it by law. The Slav colony at the east end of Braddock and the notorious Gypsy colony of Hands Court were thoroughly fumigated and disinfected. Captain Price of the Braddock Health Department went on to say, "They are cleaner now than ever before in their history." It is beyond belief that someone would make a statement like that and that a newspaper would print it. It affirmed to the other people of Braddock that the Gypsies of Hands Court were not fit for assimilation. It took over thirty years for the Gypsies of Hands Court to finally gain some dignity when a 1930s news article stated: "A report was made to the Braddock police that the Gypsies of Hands Court were trouble makers and thieves." And the Braddock police defended the Gypsies by saying, "These Gypsies have been living here for over thirty years, and we have had no major problems with them. We have far more problems with others in Braddock."

Article courtesy of the Pittsburgh Post-Gazette.

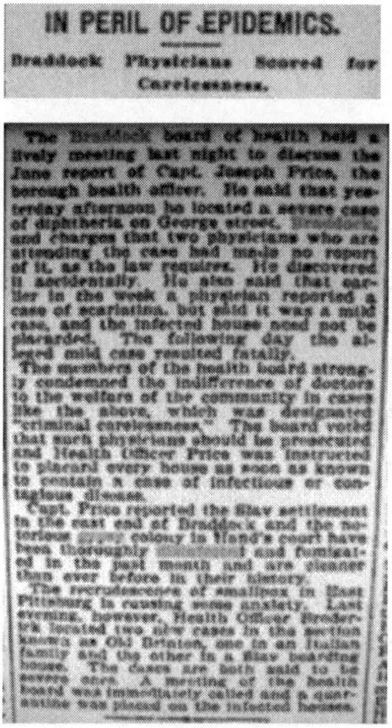

IN PERIL OF EPIDEMICS.

Braddock Physicians Scored for Carelessness.

The Braddock board of health held a lively meeting last night to discuss the June report of Capt. Joseph Price, the borough health officer. He said that yesterday afternoon he located a severe case of diphtheria on George street, Braddock, and charges that two physicians who are attending the case had made no report of it, as the law requires. He discovered it accidentally. He also said that earlier in the week a physician reported a case of scarlatina, but said it was a mild case, and the infected house need not be placarded. The following day the alleged mild case resulted fatally.

The members of the health board strongly condemned the indifference of doctors to the welfare of the community in cases like the above, which was designated "criminal carelessness." The board voted that such physicians should be prosecuted and Health Officer Price was instructed to placard every house as soon as known to contain a case of infectious or contagious disease.

Capt. Price reported the Slav settlement in the east end of Braddock and the notorious gypsy colony in Hand's court have been thoroughly cleaned and fumigated in the past month and are cleaner than ever before in their history.

The recrudescence of smallpox in East Pittsburg is causing some anxiety. Last evening, however, Health Officer Broderick located two new cases in the section known as Old Brinton, one in an Italian family and the other in a Slav boarding house. The cases are both said to be severe ones. A meeting of the health board was immediately called and a quarantine was placed on the infected houses.

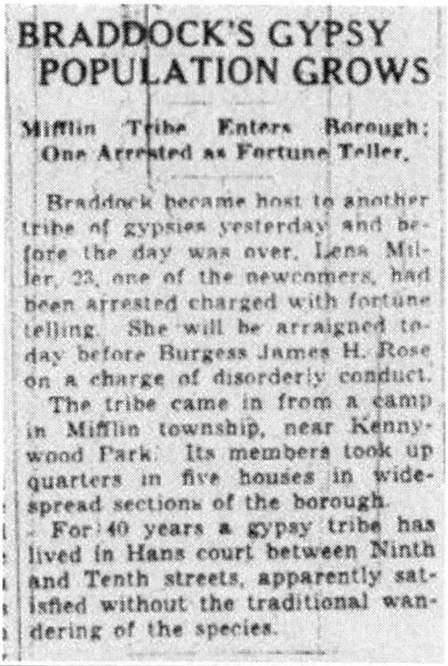

BRADDOCK'S GYPSY POPULATION GROWS

Mifflin Tribe Enters Borough; One Arrested as Fortune Teller.

Braddock became host to another tribe of gypsies yesterday and before the day was over, Lena Miller, 23, one of the newcomers, had been arrested charged with fortune telling. She will be arraigned today before Burgess James H. Rose on a charge of disorderly conduct.

The tribe came in from a camp in Mifflin township, near Kennywood Park. Its members took up quarters in five houses in widespread sections of the borough.

For 40 years a gypsy tribe has lived in Hans court between Ninth and Tenth streets, apparently satisfied without the traditional wandering of the species.

July 1, 1899 *November 19, 1934*

Braddock Gypsy Orchestra, Photograph courtesy of Tony Selepsky

Braddock Gypsy Orchestra, Photograph courtesy of Douglas Polo

There were many reporters, writers, journalists, and authors who studied Gypsies. A lot of their writing was hypothesized and embellished. All of them cited inaccuracies among each other. One was a journal written by Endre De Spur, *Gypsies in the Borough of Braddock, U.S.A.* He stated that the most notorious of these writings was Konrad Bercovici's *The Story of the Gypsies* (1928)" was imaginary data about Gypsies, not an effort to tell the story of who they were.

What he failed to mention is that Bercovici was also a fiction writer and wrote a few fiction books about Gypsy stories. His autobiography is titled *The Gypsy in Me*, and he was Jewish American. De Spur wrote in his journal: "In New York I heard the performance of a well-advertised Gypsy countess in a Hungarian dining room." He also said her playing was artistic, (referring to the Gypsy Countess Verona). When he mentioned it to another musician friend, the friend smilingly remarked that the "countess" was a pupil of his and became "gypsified" only for the time of her contract.

De Spur was a reporter writing a story about Gypsies, and he went to see a Gypsy playing, but he did not interview her; instead, he asked someone else. The Gypsy Countess Verona was a well-known musician from the group of Hungarian/Slovak Gypsies I write about in this book. De Spur also stated: "And naturally those 'pioneer' Gypsy musicians were, in general, not of the best type" (referring to the Gypsies of Braddock). This journal was written in the late 1950s to early 1960s when a few Gypsies were still living in Braddock. Again he made a statement that he couldn't back up factually because he was not there.

De Spur went on to say, "I wish I could still meet and interview some of the thousand Gypsies who moved to

Cleveland and Detroit, if they have not moved even farther on since then, but Mr. Jesensky wrote to me some time ago that he was unable to find the real interesting types in Cleveland." By this comment he meant the anthropologically characteristic types of Gypsies. De Spur was in Braddock, which is less than two and a half hours away from Cleveland, and he didn't investigate himself; he listened to someone else's opinion. He did say that the Gypsies still had something to offer to the lore, particularly to the folklore, of music.

While in Braddock, De Spur talked to Julia Margitza who told him about her sister the "Gypsy Countess Verona." Then he talked to seventy-two-year-old Mr. Pohlatko who said that Polo is the American pronunciation of the name, and he interviewed Jerry Lacy at length, who went by the name of "Kocsonya."

Then De Spur realized that these Hungarian/Slovak Gypsies were in fact the *Verbunkos* Gypsies of Hungary. *Verbunkos* was a term that described a dance type of music played by Gypsies; later the term was changed to the *czardas*.

De Spur then told Jerry (Kocsonya) Lacey that he knew and played with Racz Laci, Imre Magyari, and the Rajko Band. Then De Spur linked the Hungarian/Slovak Gypsies in America directly to Bela Radics, Imre Magyari, Sandor Bura, and Bela Berkes.

There has been much controversy over the music: is it Gypsy music or Hungarian music? Franz Liszt was well known for his recognition of Gypsy music and for his 1853 publication of *Hungarian Rhapsodies*. In his book *The Gypsies and Their Music of Hungary* (1859), he wrote that Hungarian music would amount to very little without the Gypsies. Hungarian music had been in the hands of the Gypsies since the 1760s, and Liszt was attacked for his statements. Critics of Liszt said that they did not doubt the contributions made by the "new Hungarians," (what they called the Gypsies), but they were playing Hungarian music, not Gypsy music. They said Franz Liszt did not speak Hungarian and spent most of his life elsewhere, so he was not qualified to comment on what Hungarian music was.

Mihaly Barna, was the first noted Gypsy violinist and Hungarian freedom fighter in 1737. He and Prince Francis Racokzy fought together and were exiled together in Turkey. Panna Czinka (1711–1772) was the granddaughter of Mihaly Barna. By the age of fifteen, she was leading her own Gypsy orchestra. She is credited with forming the traditional Gypsy orchestra of a *primas* (lead violinist), cimbalom, bass, and second violin. It is said that she "drew sparks from her violin bow, making the very stones shiver."

Bálint Sárosi, author of *Gypsy Music* (1978), claimed that Panna Czinka's grandfather Mihaly Barna was fictitious and that Racokzy had no Gypsies in his retinue. Janos Bihari (1764–1824) wrote over eighty compositions including the "Racokzy March." Franz Liszt was an admirer of Bihari, and he said, "Like drops of some fiery spirit essence, the notes of his magic violin came to our ears." Sarosi claimed that Bihari did not write the "Racokzy March."

Pista Danko (1858–1903) was one of the most successful Gypsy musicians; he wrote the music for over four hundred poems and wrote the "March of the Hungarians" for the thousandth anniversary of the Hungarian state in 1885. A statue of Pista Danko was erected in Szeged, Hungary, and a movie was made about his life.

Bálint Sárosi said that Panna Czinka, Janos Behari, Pista Danko, Pali Racz, and other Gypsy musicians have grown into mythical characters and have been embellished rather than documented. In 1905 Sándor Hevesi, the famous theatre director, recommended Hungarian culture rid itself of the tired romantic cult of the Gypsy. The classical violinist Ede Reményi said, "If we want our national music to be spoken of with respect in educated circles abroad, we must strive, above all, in our homeland to take our fine music out of the hands of the many frothy, chaffy, tastelessly gaudy, dilettantish, wild, and virtuoso Gypsies, whose style is an affront to a deep sense of beauty, and to elevate it from the stinking morasses of the centuries in which they had sunken and still keep on sinking it through their distorted procedures. Let us stop boasting of it. In other countries music is played in gardens, pubs, and in the streets [especially what they call "Garten Musik"], yet no one would think of saying that such catchpenny musical literature was real art."

Look at these dates:
Mihaly Barna (b 17th century d.?)
Panna Czinka (1711–1772)
Janos Bihari (1764–1827)
Niccolo Paganini (1782–1840)
Franz Liszt (1811–1886)
Ede Remenyi (1828–1898)
Pista Danko (1858–1903)
Béla Bartók (1881–1945)
Zoltán Kodály (1882–1967)

Zoltán Kodály and Béla Bartók, at the height of their careers, said the same thing about the Gypsies that Sándor Hevesi, Ede Reményi, and Blaint Sorosi had said about the

Gypsy musicians. Kodaly recognized the Gypsy musician, while Bartok shunned them. On May 29, 1930, in a football stadium in Budapest, a concert was held with one thousand Gypsy musicians. The famous novelist Zsigmond Móricz said, "Hey Gypsy, dog Gypsy you ... you played the country away." It is well known that the royalty of Europe had their own Gypsy musicians. Queen Elizabeth's favorite song was a Gypsy song, and the entire British royal family loved Gypsy music. Francis Joseph had a favorite Gypsy song.

The Archduke Joseph had a Gypsy musician named Marci Banda. Prime Minister Istvan Tisza's favorite Gypsy musician was Imre Magyari. And there were many more connections between royalty and Gypsy musicians. The Rajko School of Music opened in 1952 in Budapest; *Rajko* in Hungarian means "young Gypsy." The school is still open for young Gypsies to learn traditional music.

Much more has been written on this subject. Those Hungarians who would not acknowledge the Gypsy musicians also said, "Gypsy musicians were not capable of writing Hungarian music; they only played what they were taught."

The definition of a cimbalom in the *Encyclopedia Britannica* is: "An elaborate stringed instrument of the dulcimer family used in small music ensembles by central European Roma (Gypsies); it is the national instrument of Hungary."

For hundreds of years, Gypsies played their music in thousands of restaurants, nightclubs, and taverns in Hungary. One did not go into those places to hear Zoltán Kodály or Béla Bartók music; one did not go into those places to hear Ede Reményi play. Sándor Hevesi did not have to direct the Gypsies on how to play. Zsigmond Móricz was a loyalist Hungarian and was not qualified to speak about Gypsies, and Bálint Sárosi, along with all the rest of the Hungarians who refused to acknowledge the Gypsies, is "wishful thinking." In Hungarian Gypsy music, the name says it all, one went with the other, and today, Gypsy orchestras still play the songs of Jonas Bihari and Pista Danko.

The Gypsies did adapt to the music of the country they migrated to. Their talent was to a level that they took the country's music and refined it to a point that it became their own; not only in Hungary, but also in Spain, France, Romania, Slovakia, Turkey, and Bulgaria.

Throughout the years there were many funerals. Gypsies from all the communities would come together to grieve. Typically a funeral would last three to four days, and there was always a lot of music, food, and drink. On the morning of the funeral, musicians would gather to play. Sometimes as many as fifty to seventy-five musicians would play. The music was sad and slow, in the fashion of the *halgato*, a Hungarian term for slow Gypsy music.

Braddock Funeral 1930s
Photographs from the Gus Horvath Collection

Gypsies from Homestead and Braddock attended this funeral around 1930. Gypsies from other communities are also present. There are few Gypsies left who could identify everyone in the picture, which I got from the Catholic Diocese of Pittsburgh. They said it was not uncommon for the individual churches to take photographs like this.

The Gypsy funeral became an important part of the documentation of this particular group of Gypsies, as you will see throughout this book. The pictures span their entire time in the U.S. Some of the pictures in this book are not the best quality; so we did what we could. Most of the pictures are the only ones that exist; so it's even more important to include them.

There would be ten or more *primas* (lead violin player), each taking a turn to play, with the most respected one leading the orchestra. Other *gadjo* (non-Gypsy) musicians were amazed by how these Gypsies could come together and sound like a symphony. They played traditional songs throughout the funeral. "Soven, Soven chave mamangen miro bo ogif zeleno odad mulias"-"Sleep, children, sleep, do not ask for bread; the wheat is green and father is dead." These are the words to one of the most played Gypsy songs at a funeral. There was a song

30 Violins Intone Requiem for King of Gypsy Fiddlers

P D OCT 22 '48

BRADDOCK, Pa., Oct. 21—(AP)—Gypsy violins sang a sad farewell today to Andrew Margitza, a king of the gypsy fiddlers. It was fulfillment of his dying wishes.

On his deathbed, Margitza asked that "the old musicians, the young and the very young" play for him as his casket was lowered into the ground.

The unwritten music sobbing from the violins was:

"I am going to leave you forever."

That haunting melody was passed down through generations of gypsies. The old violin maestro bequeathed it to his sons while his fingers still were agile to the bow.

The 60-year-old Margitza died Sunday.

His sons, Julius of Detroit, and Louis of Chicago, led 30 violinists in the bitter-sweet requiem.

It was a colorful Romany tradition. More than a thousand friends watched and listened.

The musical procession wended from the Margitza home to St. Michael's Catholic Church. Thence to the cemetery.

There atop a windy hill, Margitza's casket was re-opened. His sons moved forward with their violens. Then the casket was closed.

This article of Andrew Margitza's funeral (1948 in Braddock) names the funeral march and says it was passed down through generations of Gypsies. Article courtesy of The Cleveland Press Collection, Cleveland State University for an older person and a younger person, or they would play the deceased person's favorite song. The Gypsies followed the Jewish Shiva custom of covering the mirrors during the funeral, this custom stopped about 40 years ago, when the heritage started to fall apart. There were many funerals where the casket was in the home of the deceased, and not in a funeral parlor.

When the casket was closed, and the pallbearers began to carry the body out to the hearse, they played a dirge (funeral march). Some of the Gypsies say the name of the song is "I Am Leaving You Forever;" others say it is called "To Dirt." This is a very beautiful song that has been played at these Gypsy funerals for well over a hundred years that we know of. No one remembers who wrote the song or when this tradition started. This is the only song in Gypsy history that has never been recorded. There is no sheet music for it. The only time it can be played is at a funeral. The only time a musician can learn the song is at a funeral. Gypsies will not even think of the melody. The song was passed down through generations and generations of musicians.

There have been claims as to who wrote the "dirge" all of them are unfounded. I found many references to the funeral dirge throughout the years the Hungarian Gypsies have been in America. No newspaper article ever cited a composer of the song. The Gypsies who claim they know who wrote the dirge were alive when the articles were saying it was passed down from generation to generation and from father to son. If they wrote the funeral march, it would have said so in the newspapers throughout the history of the Hungarians Gypsies in America. With the threat of the tradition being lost today, a group of musicians have decided to record the dirge for preservation for future generations, and soon it will be the only way they can play the funeral march at funerals.

Alex Shandor and Rudy Bundzik
Photo Courtesy of Tony Selepsky

Braddock and Homestead Gypsies, Circa 1930s
Photos Courtesy of George Batyi

After the casket was loaded into the hearse, the mourners proceeded to the church. The musicians followed behind the hearse, and family and friends followed behind the musicians.

They walked for several blocks, still playing the dirge, until they arrived at the church. Today a funeral procession is a common sight. We have all seen one: the security car and/or the hearse in the front, the limo behind the hearse, and many cars behind the limo, often bedecked with funeral flags. Now add fifty Gypsy musicians all playing and another fifty to one hundred people walking on a main street, stopping all traffic, with dozens of onlookers standing on the sidewalks. I recently visited Braddock and stopped by the Carnegie Library of Braddock (the first one built in the country). The librarian told me that the residents, who still live in Braddock when the Gypsies lived there, often come to the library to find out what happened to the Gypsies. They remember the funerals. There has not been a traditional Gypsy funeral in Braddock for over forty years. After the church, they all went to the cemetery where the musicians played one last time for the deceased.

In the larger communities of Braddock, Cleveland, Detroit, and Chicago, the funerals often made it into the newspapers. The Associated Press distributed some of the funeral articles, which meant they were printed in newspapers all over the world.

In November of 1935, the death announcement of William Garber was in newspapers across the country. "King of the Gypsy Musicians is Buried in Braddock" They reported that forty Gypsy musicians played their dirge while hundreds of Gypsies filled Braddock Avenue as they mourned the death of Garber, who was well known by all Gypsies. Garber studied in Boston and New York, played with the Pittsburgh Symphony, and spent large engagements in St. Louis, Washington, Youngstown, Uniontown, and Erie. A personal friend of Fritz

Kreisler, Garber composed many elegies (a short, pensive musical composition) typical of his people. He had a son, William Garber Jr., who also became a famous musician. He made many records and was well respected in the Gypsy community; he passed away in the 1970s.

In the early 1940s, Nancy Ballog went back to Braddock to visit her grandmother, Mary Kallao of Talbot Avenue. At eighteen years old she suffered a fatal heart attack, and her funeral was in the newspapers, too. Her parents, Mr. and Mrs. Alex Ballog of Chicago, said Nancy had returned for a reunion with school friends made while she attended Braddock's First Ward School. An uncle, Rudy Ballog, of Detroit said, "We feel the music should accompany the spirit of the departed to the next world." Nineteen violinists led the orchestra. Gypsies from all of the communities attended.

Braddock Funeral 1940s
Photograph from the Gus Horvath Collection

From the left front row: Blimps Batyi
Gus Piskor, and George Batyi
Left back row: Sonny Batyi, Julius Piskor, and Cisko Batyi,
Photo property of the author.

GYPSY TUNES MARK GIRL'S BURIAL RITES

Picture on Page 17.

In accordance with age-old custom, Nancy Bellog, 18, yesterday made her last earthly journey to the melodies of Gypsy violin music.

The slight, dark girl was fatally stricken with a heart attack five days ago while visiting her grandmother, Mrs. Mary Kallao of 929 Talbot St., Braddock.

Her parents, Mr. and Mrs. Alex Ballog of Chicago, tearfully told how Nancy had returned for a reunion with school friends made while she attended Braddock's First Ward School.

An uncle, Rudy Ballog of Detroit, explained the music as Gypsy ritual. He said:

"We feel that music should accompany the spirit of the departed to the next world."

From the door of the home to St. Michael's Church, and then almost to Catholic Cemetery, the cortege was led by a band of 19 violinists, relatives who came from Detroit, Chicago and New York as well as from local points.

Nancy Ballog Funeral, June 10, 1946

The casket is not in a hearse. You can see it behind the women marching. The funeral procession continued down Braddock Avenue to St. Michael's Church. Articles Courtesy of the Pittsburgh Post-Gazette.

Willie Garber, the "Gypsy Devil," so called for his amazing violin technique, acknowledged king of local gypsy musicians, was borne to his grave yesterday through Braddock's main streets, to the mournful sound of an old gypsy funeral march. A stringed orchestra of 40 pieces lead the way from his home in the gypsy section on Hakel street to St. Michael's Church and thence after mass to the cemetery. The musicians are shown above marching up Braddock avenue.

King of Gypsy Musicians Is Buried in Braddock

40 Stringed Instruments Play Dirge While Strange Chants Are Sang by Romany Mourners For Willie Zarber.

Strange gypsy chants rose in the streets of Braddock yesterday morning, mingling with the mournful strains of 40 stringed instruments, playing the unwritten gypsy funeral march, handed down from father to son.

Willie Garber, the king of gypsy musicians, was being buried, and friends, pupils and former orchestra mates were at hand to play him to his last resting place in traditional style.

Heading the funeral procession was Louis Rokocai, the orchestra conductor, followed by four lines of violinists, a row of saxophones, one of 'cellos, more violins and just ahead of the bier a line of bass-viola, the front ends carried by small boys.

The widow, her two children, Junior, 8, and Edna, 6, and Gerber's parents, led the mourners, keening and singing.

Starting in the small house at 916 Halket avenue, where Garber died Sunday, the cortege crossed the Baltimore & Ohio Railroad tracks, and traveled several blocks through Braddock's main section.

Garber was universally known among gypsies for his ability in playing gypsy and Hungarian music and for his reputation for composing music too hard to play. He was well known to Fritz Kreisler and was looking forward to the Viennese violinist's appearance in the Mosque tomorrow.

Born near Vienna, he studied in Boston and New York, and spent long periods playing in St. Louis, Washington, Youngstown, Uniontown and Erie. Theaters in Pittsburgh knew him well in the days before the talkies when he played in the Blackstone, the Nixon, the Braddock Capitol and others.

Billy Garber Sr. Funeral 1935
Article Courtesy of the Pittsburgh Post-Gazette

All funerals are sad, but one funeral in Braddock would make you shed a tear just thinking about it. The funeral of Albert Horvath (age twenty) of Braddock passed away in December of 1939 from pneumonia, following an operation for a serious sinus condition. He was set to marry Irene Garber, twenty-one. Just before he died, he begged his mother to promise that his funeral would become his wedding. On the morning of the funeral, the musicians and the wedding party gathered. The bride wore her wedding dress, ushers donned tuxedos, bridesmaids wore gowns, and two little girls carried the bride's train while the ring bearer followed. After the service at the funeral parlor, the procession started down Braddock Avenue. An orchestra of twenty-five Gypsy musicians led the way, playing the funeral dirge. The hearse followed behind them, and then came the bride with the little girls carrying her train. As the bride walked behind the hearse, she wept while trying to make it look like she was getting married. The bridesmaids and ushers walked behind her. After the church services at St. Michaels, the procession proceeded again down Braddock Avenue, moving very slowly. It took about thirty minutes to walk just a few blocks. At the cemetery, the bride dropped her bouquet of roses onto the casket as it was lowered. Albert and Irene had been friends since childhood.

December 1939

Gypsy Violins Play—

Wedding Becomes Funeral, Bridal Corsage a Wreath

◆ ◆ ◆

Bridegroom - to - Be's Last Wishes Carried Out At Services

By JOHN TROAN

The "bride" was there—in a flowing snow-white gown with a corsage of roses.

So were the "bridesmaids"—all eight of them—and a half-dozen "ushers."

But instead of marching to the rhythm of the "Wedding March," Irene Garber walked slowly, head down, her feet dragging to the sad tones of a gypsy funeral dirge.

Albert Horvath—the man she was to marry—had died. But they were carrying out his last wish.

"If I die before I can get married," he said on his deathbed, "please carry out the wedding at my funeral."

All their lives Albert and Irene had been close friends. They were born within a year of each other. As children, they played together, romped to school together.

Albert reached his 20th birthday anniversary. Irene was a year older. They decided to marry.

Then a few months ago, Albert suddenly developed a serious tonsil condition. He underwent an operation and two weeks ago he left his bed.

But a cold set him back again. It turned to pneumonia. Early Thursday Albert died.

Today, from Albert's late home at [illegible] Tenth St., Braddock, to St. Michael's Church, at Eleventh St. and Braddock Ave., the "wedding procession" wound.

About 25 gypsy musicians, most of them with typical violin and bow, led the procession. In the next row, two cellists marched. Between them was a vacant "post."

That's where Albert should have been. He was a cellist.

Then, with three train-bearers,

Article Courtesy of the Pittsburgh Post-Gazette

GYPSY 'WEDDING' BECOMES FUNERAL

(Continued From Page One)

came Irene, the bridesmaids, the ushers—in front of the hearse.

After a 35-minute ceremony in the church, the procession formed again. The march was slow now—it took almost a half-hour to go five blocks. Traffic stalled.

The musicians disbanded, and funeral cars went to the Braddock Catholic Cemetery, North Braddock, about a mile away.

Once again, the train-bearers trailed behind Irene, her roses fluttering in a slight breeze.

The casket was borne to its grave. From "nowhere," a group of musicians appeared. Violins played the notes of a staccato-like dirge.

The casket was lowered.

Then just as suddenly as it had started, the music stopped. Irene looked at her corsage.

She tossed it atop the casket.

Bride-To-Be Again

IRENE GARBER

This time, to the altar.

◆ ◆ ◆

Gypsy Bride, Death Balked, To Try Again

Irene Garber marched again as a bride-to-be—but this time more in the spirit of the season.

It was the week before Christmas, while gypsy violins played a funeral dirge, that Irene first marched in the white gown of a bride.

Her head bowed, she walked slowly to the grave of her intended bridegroom—20-year-old Albert Horvath, in fulfillment of his deathbed wish:

"If I die before I can get married, please carry out the wedding at my funeral."

Yesterday, true to the spirit of Leap Year Day, Irene marched again—from her home in Tenth St., Braddock, to the Marriage License Bureau in the County Courthouse.

Her husband-to-be is Max Bandy of Chicago.

1940

Bride, Wedding Party, Walk With Death

A white-clad "bride" with a corsage of roses, followed by train bearers, "bridesmaids" and "ushers," followed the casket of Albert Horvath when he was buried at Pittsburgh, Pa. The "bride," Irene Garber, who was to have married Horvath, complied with his dying request to, "Please carry out the wedding at my funeral." The strange "wedding" party, above, walked to the tune of a dirge by Gypsy musicians with one vacant place in their ranks—Horvath's. He was stricken with pneumonia while planning for the wedding.

Articles Courtesy of the Pittsburgh Post-Gazette

Braddock/Detroit Gypsies
Photos Courtesy of George Batyi

Julka Polo, Louis (Poodie) Krista, Antie Philips, and Greenie Polo

At a funeral in 1940 for Louis Garber Jr., forty Gypsy musicians played as the procession went down Braddock Avenue. Hundreds of residents of he town lined Braddock Avenue to view the funeral. Louis Jr. died in Detroit and was taken to Braddock where his father Louis Garber had lived. His brothers were Boldy, Lotzie, Joe, William, and Frank.

One of the most-publicized funerals was that of Andrew Margitza. I found about forty articles in newspapers across the United States. Margitza passed away in 1948. His wife was Julia (Miko), his son was the famous Gypsy violinist Ziggy Bela, whose real name was Julius Margitza. His other children were Louis (Kalo), William (Texas), Alex, Irene, Helen, Mildred, and Martha. His dying wish was to have his grandsons, Julius and Richard, play for his funeral.

On the morning of the funeral, about forty Gypsy musicians played, including Ziggy's son Julius and Louis' son Richard, both about fourteen years old.

Other noted musicians who played at his funeral were George Polatka, Frank Garber, and Dave Ballog. This was one of the most-talented Gypsy families, and they would go on to produce a long line of famous musicians. Andrew's grandson Julius had a long and famous career in jazz; his recording name was Julio Bela. Grandson Richard went on to play

PITTSBURGH POST-GAZETTE
WEDNESDAY, DECEMBER 20, 1939

Girl Wears Wedding Dress For Funeral of Her Fiance

Old Gypsy Custom Observed as Bride-to-Be Walks Behind Hearse in Braddock Streets.

In the white gown and veil she had ready for her wedding, Irene Garber, 21, yesterday walked through the streets of Braddock behind the hearse bearing the body of her fiance, Albert Horvath, 20.

Just before he died Thursday, Albert begged his mother to promise that according to gypsy custom, his funeral would become his wedding.

And so it was. In his home in Braddock's gypsy court in Tenth and Halket streets, the "wedding" party gathered yesterday morning, ushers in tuxedos, bridesmaids in gowns of blue and yellow silk, two little white clad train bearers, and a ring bearer.

After a brief service, the coffin was carried to a hearse. Then the procession moved slowly from Tenth street to St. Michael's Church at Eleventh street and Braddock avenue.

A band of 25 gypsy musicians led the way, their violins playing slow, mournful gypsy funeral music. Behind them came the hearse. Then came the bride, two little girls carrying her long white train. She tried to hold her head up, proudly as though this were really her wedding. But now and then her chin would sink and a tear would streak down her cheek. Behind her walked the bridesmaids and ushers.

After services in St. Michael's Church, the procession formed again, this time marching so slowly that it required a half hour to march five blocks. Funeral cars then took the marchers to Braddock Catholic cemetery.

There was another dirge at the cemetery as the casket was lowered. Then Irene stepped to the graveside and dropped her boquet of roses onto the casket top.

Her fiance developed pneumonia, following an operation for a serious sinus condition. He and Irene, both members of the Braddock gypsy colony, had been friends since childhood.

PITTSBURGH SUN-TELEGRAPH
MONDAY, FEBRUARY 26, 1940

40 Gypsies Play Violin Dirge In Braddock Funeral March

Louis Garber, Jr., Granted Last Wish For Native Music

An ancient Hungarian Gypsy funeral dirge, "To Dirt," was played today by more than 40 Gypsy violinists at the funeral march for Louis Garber, Jr., 27, a member of the Braddock clan of Gypsies.

The procession, with the violin players in front, slowly moved to the St. Michael's Church, Braddock Avenue. Crowds of Braddock citizens lined the four-block procession to the church.

Musicians from Cleveland, Detroit and New York played for Louis Garber, who was a well-known violinist among Gypsy circles.

Garber died in Detroit on Tuesday. His body was brought to the home of his father, Louis Garber, at 916 Halket Avenue, Braddock, an elder of the Gypsy tribe which has made its headquarters in Braddock for five years.

After solemn high mass in St. Michael's Church the funeral procession moved slowly through the heart of Braddock to the Roman Catholic Cemetery. All along the line of march the violins murmured the tune handed down from generation to generation.

Louis Garber, Jr., leaves his parents, five brothers, Baldy, Lotzie, Frank, Joe and William Bela, and a sister, Mrs. Ida Kalov.

A DIRGE

Playing Violins At Gypsy Rites

Articles Courtesy of the Pittsburgh Post-Gazette

SECOND SECTION
FRIDAY,
OCT. 22, 1948

Pittsburgh Post-Gazette

Strains of Native Song Say Last Farewell to Violinist

Gypsy Has His Music Even in Death

Leader Given Type of Burial He Had Wanted

By Eugene F. Jacobi

Sons of Andrew Margitza play a gypsy farewell over his grave as other relatives, friends mourn the dead musician.

Woman Sings Way Out of Jail

The funeral of Andrew Margitza was published in the Pittsburgh Post-Gazette and the Pittsburgh Sun-Telegraph on October nineteenth and twenty-first of 1948. The Associated Press distributed this funeral notice. The main newspapers that covered stories of these Gypsies were from Pittsburgh, Cleveland, Detroit, Youngstown, and Chicago. The newspapers often covered funerals as well as weddings and baptisms. Reporters and journalists from all over the world were writing stories about Gypsies.
Article Courtesy of the Pittsburgh Post-Gazette

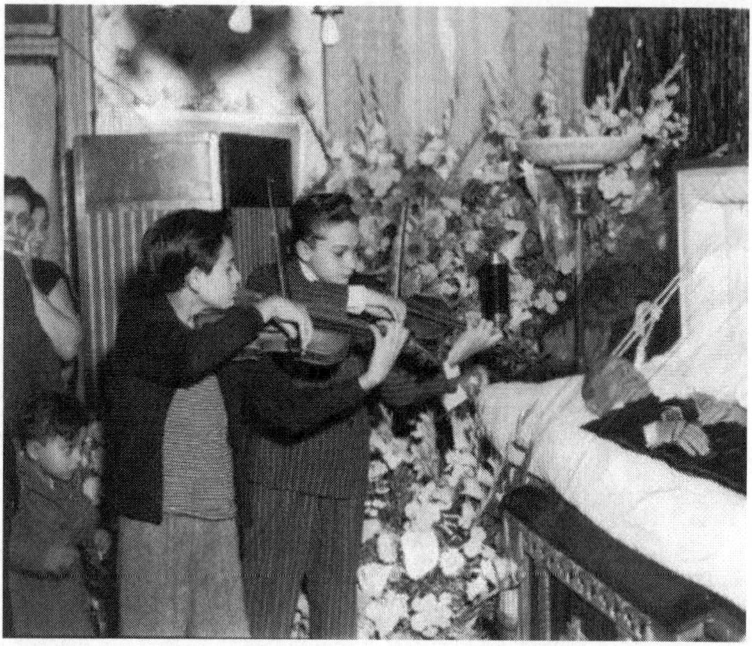

Julka and Richie Margitza
Photo Courtesy of the Pittsburgh Post-Gazette

Braddock Funeral 1930s
Photo Courtesy of the Pittsburgh Post-Gazette

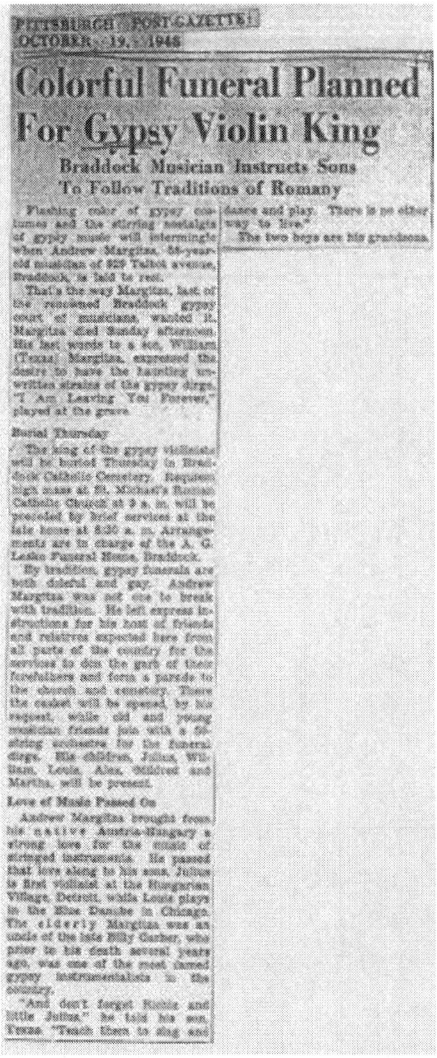

PITTSBURGH POST-GAZETTE
OCTOBER 19, 1948

Colorful Funeral Planned For Gypsy Violin King

Braddock Musician Instructs Sons To Follow Traditions of Romany

Flashing color of gypsy costumes and the stirring nostalgia of gypsy music will intermingle when Andrew Margitza, 58-year-old musician of 829 Talbot avenue, Braddock, is laid to rest.

That's the way Margitza, last of the renowned Braddock gypsy court of musicians, wanted it. Margitza died Sunday afternoon. His last words to a son, William (Texas) Margitza, expressed the desire to have the haunting unwritten strains of the gypsy dirge, "I Am Leaving You Forever," played at the grave.

Burial Thursday

The king of the gypsy violinists will be buried Thursday in Braddock Catholic Cemetery. Requiem high mass at St. Michael's Roman Catholic Church at 9 a. m. will be preceded by brief services at the late home at 8:30 a. m. Arrangements are in charge of the A. G. Lesko Funeral Home, Braddock.

By tradition, gypsy funerals are both doleful and gay. Andrew Margitza was not one to break with tradition. He left express instructions for his host of friends and relatives expected here from all parts of the country for the services to don the garb of their forefathers and form a parade to the church and cemetery. There the casket will be opened, by his request, while old and young musician friends join with a 50-string orchestra for the funeral dirge. His children, Julius, William, Louis, Alex, Mildred and Martha, will be present.

Love of Music Passed On

Andrew Margitza brought from his native Austria-Hungary a strong love for the music of stringed instruments. He passed that love along to his sons. Julius is first violinist at the Hungarian Village, Detroit, while Louis plays in the Blue Danube in Chicago. The elderly Margitza was an uncle of the late Billy Garber, who prior to his death several years ago, was one of the most famed gypsy instrumentalists in the country.

"And don't forget Richie and little Julius," he told his son, Texas. "Teach them to sing and dance and play. There is no other way to live."

The two boys are his grandsons.

Strings in Dirge at Gypsy Violinist's Burial

The funeral of Andrew Margitza was one of the most-publicized funerals. I have found over forty articles in newspaper across the country.
October 22, 1948
Article Courtesy of the Pittsburgh Post-Gazette

for the Detroit Symphony, and he was one of the personal violin players for Motown records. Julius' (Julio) son, Randy Margitza, is a symphony violin player and traveled with Andrew Lloyd Webber's *Phantom of the Opera*. Richard's son is the famous saxophone player, Rick Margitza, whose career started with Miles Davis, and to date he has eighty-one sessions listed on the discography.

In 1967 William Margitza died (better known as "Texas"). He owned the Texas Hotel and tavern in Braddock on Talbot Avenue, across from the "Braddock yard." Texas ran for the Braddock city Council in 1947. This was one of three funerals I had the opportunity to attend in Braddock as a young boy in the '60s. The body was laid out inside the tavern, and Gypsies from all of the communities attended.

In 1920 Prohibition started, which banned alcohol and launched the roaring '20s. You would think this law would have hurt the Gypsies since they played mostly in taverns, but it didn't. Along with Prohibition came organized crime and bootlegging. Gangsters in Chicago, such as Al Capone, started to manufacture illegal whiskey, and people wanted it more than when it was legal. For 13 years millions of Americans were drinking illegal whiskey. The law was repealed in 1933.

The cupboards are bare and there's little prospect of relief in the Braddock gypsy colony, where the men are musicians and the women dance, for there has been no call for the services of the band. Upper picture shows a girl-mother with her baby and at work, and below is a youngster of the colony with one of the few musical instruments that have escaped the pawnshops.

Article Courtesy of the Pittsburgh Post-Gazette

HARD TIMES HIT ROMANY

Lack of Call for Music Leaves Cupboards Bare in Gypsy Colony

150 FAM... CHRISTMAS ...

HARD TIMES HIT ROMANY

Continued from Page 1. This Section school here in Braddock. But sometimes they can't go because they have no shoes."

The gypsies tell the story of their own need. Shoes are supplied some of them every three months by the schools. They would not attend school otherwise.

No Meals Christmas

"On Christmas Day nobody in this house had a bite to eat," said Mrs. Frank Kobotsky. "My husband has not been able to work for three years. My mother-in-law is old. She has no shoes. She has to wear old felt slippers somebody gave her. We have three children under 8. See my cupboard. This is all I have to eat." She produced a half-emptied milk bottle. "That is all I have in the house to give these six people for supper tonight."

A survey of the Gypsy colony was made by E. L. Mossler, Pittsburgh business man who is aiding the colony.

"I found conditions as pitiful as they were in France and Belgium after the occupation," Mossler said. "There are 130 in the colony. Rents are long overdue. There are doctor bills due. Some 30 tons of coal will be needed to tide them over till spring."

January 4, 1931

October 29, 1929, is known as Black Tuesday, the day the stock market crashed and the Great Depression began. Everyone in America, as well as the rest of the world, was affected by it. The Gypsies made it through the Depression by sticking together and helping each other. Musicians helped each other by playing music jobs to make sure everyone had food on the table. One family could not feed the whole community, but the community could feed one family.

An article in the *Pittsburgh Press* tells of how hard the Depression hit the Gypsies in Braddock. It was the harshest winter the twenty-seven families of Hands Court had survived since first moving to Braddock thirty-five years earlier. Louis Duda, father of eight children, said, "Most of the men are naturalized. All of the children were born in this country. We had three soldiers in the World War and one of the soldiers went to France."

"On Christmas Day no one in this house had a bite to eat," said Mrs. Frank Kolbasky.

I can remember some of the older Gypsies talking about how hard it was. They said their mothers would make something to eat out of nothing; they would eat sugar bread; and they could buy something for a penny. They told stories about waiting for coal trains to pass by so that they could have a few pieces of coal for their stoves.

Gypsy Lovers in Gay Colors And Spangles Head Strange Wedding March in Braddock

Spirited Tunes of [illegible] Keep Time for Participants in Pageant—Youthful Bride and Bridegroom Betrothed Since Birth.

Dressed in native costumes and marching to the spirited tunes of Romany the strangest bridal couple seen in Braddock in many a day marched to the altar yesterday. Bride and bridegroom were each 15 years old and, according to the ancient custom of their race, had been betrothed since birth.

Hands Court, [illegible] is a bit of Romany transplanted to American soil. Its inhabitants are Gypsies. Louis Franko and Margaret Caleu were the principals of the wedding. Both were born in the little colony of musicians.

Many persons paused to watch the wedding procession as it wended its way through the rain from the court to St. Michael's Church, Braddock avenue. The gay colors worn by the women and the men in full dress regalia presented a strange spectacle. Although the wedding is over the festivities will not come to an end until tomorrow night.

June 28, 1919; Wedding of Louis Fransco to Margaret Kallao, both fifteen years old and betrothed to each other since birth, the men and women dressed in gay colors presented a strange spectacle.

Gypsies

By WILLIAM M. KIMMEL

Post-Gazette Staff Writer

LANDMARKS familiar to thousands are vanishing from the scene as wrecking crews change the face of the city and surrounding communities. Only a handful note the passing of the old places. The others hurry on.

One such landmark was Han's Court in Braddock, now the site of Talbot Towers, a low rental housing project. For years a colony of Hungarian gypsy musicians lived in the ramshackle frame houses that made up the court.

Mr. Kimmel

Their patriarch was Andy Margitza, a Hungarian musician who earned his livelihood playing and teaching the violin.

Unlike other gypsies, the colony spurned horse trading and fortune telling and lived solely by music. In good times the men would play in the district's hotels and night clubs. In bad times they stayed in their homes passing the secrets of gypsy music to the children. When one of the colony passed away hundreds of gypsies from all over the country gathered to mourn.

* * *

There was always the traditional binding of the dead person's mouth to keep him or her from revealing gypsy secrets, and the binding of the feet so he wouldn't become a nomad in time.

* * *

And on the day of the funeral the men and women donned costumes of brilliant red and gold for the march to the cemetery.

Hundreds gathered to watch the procession wind through Braddock's streets, while as many as 100 fiddlers played R[illegible] tunes, some gay and some sad.

During the depression the WPA organized the gypsies into a string band and they gave concerts throughout the county.

* * *

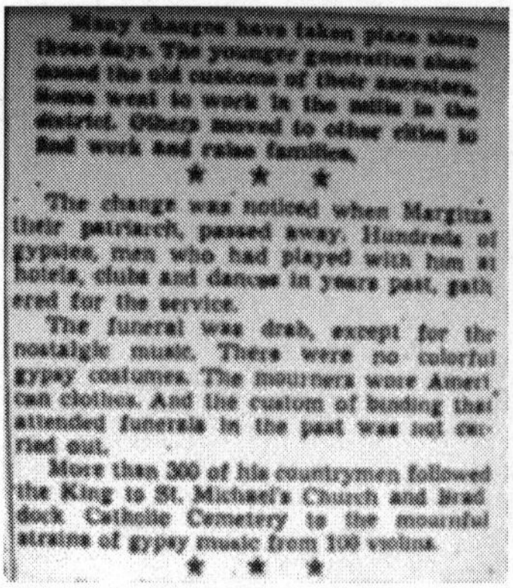

Many changes have taken place since those days. The younger generation abandoned the old customs of their ancestors. Some went to work in the mills in the district. Others moved to other cities to find work and raise families.

* * *

The change was noticed when Margitza their patriarch, passed away. Hundreds of gypsies, men who had played with him at hotels, clubs and dances in years past, gathered for the service.

The funeral was drab, except for the nostalgic music. There were no colorful gypsy costumes. The mourners wore American clothes. And the custom of binding that attended funerals in the past was not carried out.

More than 300 of his countrymen followed the King to St. Michael's Church and Braddock Catholic Cemetery to the mournful strains of gypsy music from 100 violins.

* * *

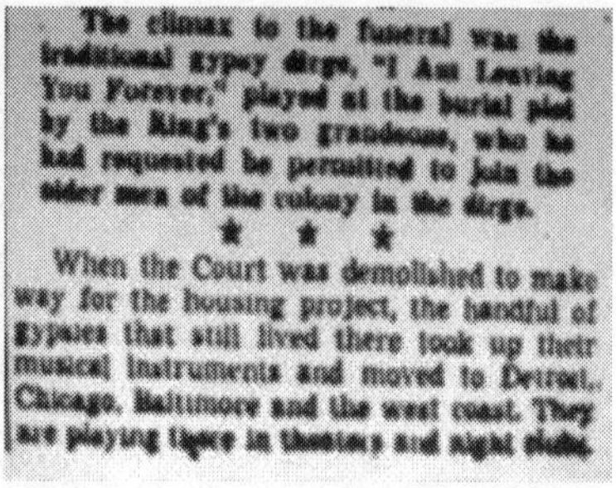

The climax to the funeral was the traditional gypsy dirge, "I Am Leaving You Forever," played at the burial plot by the King's two grandsons, who he had requested be permitted to join the older men of the colony in the dirge.

* * *

When the Court was demolished to make way for the housing project, the handful of gypsies that still lived there took up their musical instruments and moved to Detroit, Chicago, Baltimore and the west coast. They are playing there in theaters and night clubs.

Article written in the 1960s about the Gypsies of "Hands court", says they did the traditional binding of the mouth and feet to the deceased to keep them from revealing secrets and wandering. The men and women dressed in bright colors of red and gold. Just more stereotyping from a clueless reporter.
Article Courtesy of the Pittsburgh Post-Gazette

In the 1930s the government started the Works Progress Administration, better known as the WPA, to try and restart the economy. Money was allocated to place specific groups who were out of work and get professionals back to work. One such group was musicians, and WPA orchestras were formed all over the country. In Cleveland there were a few Gypsy members. In Chicago there was a five-piece Gypsy orchestra. In Braddock the entire thirty-two-member orchestra was Gypsy. The Braddock WPA orchestra became one of the most popular WPA orchestras ever assembled.

The Braddock WPA orchestra consisted of all Gypsies, marching down Braddock Avenue, for the 175th anniversary of the Defeat of Braddock, 1930.
Photo Courtesy of the Braddock Historical Society

addock Gypsies Who Live By Violins Helped By WPA

PRESS

Braddock Colony Spurns Fortune Telling To Follow Music

P&L W.P.A.

FEB 19 1936

The gypsies of Braddock have turned thumbs down on fortune telling.

The men ow the miniature colony —there are only about two dozen families—have remained loyal to the tradition of their Hungarian ancestors, who loved music with passionate devotion.

Joined together today in a 32-piece orchestra, they are giving free concerts throughout the city under sponsorship of the Works Progress Administration. They claim to be the only all-gypsy musical unit in America organized under the Federal Government work-relief program.

"We are music-loving gypsies," said Alex Bogar, who plays the Dulcimer in the orchestra, and acts as master of ceremonies.

"What do I think of fortune telling? It is too low for us. We don't know that business. We have nothing to do with fortune tellers.

"We are Hungarian gypsies, from a land that now belongs to Czechoslovakia. We make our living by playing our violins so they reach your heart.

"Always, when one of our children is about four years old, he is given a three-quarter size fiddle, and we start teaching him the old Magyar airs.

"What would I think of one of our men who did not want to be a musician? I would think he did not want to be a gypsy."

Mr. Bogar lives at 906 Halket Ave. The conductor of the orchestra is Michael Bandy. The players memorize all the numbers for their concerts, because they say "music must come from the heart, not from the sheet of music."

They have found that the public always enjoy their playing of the czardas, native gypsy dance music. Another group of the gypsies, about one dozen families, lives in Homestead.

Article Courtesy of the Pittsburgh Post-Gazette

Michael Bandy was the conductor of the orchestra; one of the cimbalom players was Alex Bogar. The orchestra's life was cut short when regulations were passed requiring all members of the orchestra to read music. Since most of the Gypsies played by ear, about twenty members were cut, leaving a small Gypsy orchestra. Eventually all but two were cut: Andrew Goldie, string bass, and William Horvath, cellist. When the Gypsies were cut from the orchestra, they left without saying a word and accepted the situation out of fear of retaliation if they spoke against it. When it comes to music that grips your heart, many declare that there isn't a race in the world that can surpass the Gypsies.

In 1939 the Depression ended and World War II started in Europe. Americans knew that it was only a matter of time before they entered the war. There were a few Gypsy men who served in WWI. Many Gypsy men served in the armed forces during World War II, the Korean War, and Vietnam War, too. My mother's three brothers and my father's two brothers all enlisted. In the 1940s it was a common sight to see Gypsy men in uniform. A few of them were awarded the Purple Heart.

My mother said that when she was just a child, the news came out about the atrocities that Adolph Hitler was committing against the Gypsies. She told me, "I can remember my father reading the newspaper and crying." She had asked him, "Dad why are you crying?" And he had replied, "He's killing our people." All the Gypsies could do was cry and pray that someone would put an end to Adolph Hitler.

Left front row: Frank Kish, Louis (Lajos) Ballog in WWII uniform, Louis (Bum) Ballog and back row: Adolph Ballog.

Front left: Dolly Ballog, Rita Rigo, Rudy Goldie (in Korea), and Mitzi Piskor
Photos are the property of the author.

Braddock and Homestead Gypsies Circa 1950
Braddock and Homestead were less than three miles apart.
Youngstown was less than an hour and a half away.
Cleveland was about two and a half hours away.
Photo property of the author

The only Gypsies by presidential appointment to sit on the United States Holocaust Memorial Council were Bill Duna and Professor Ian Hancock Ph.D... Duna's family was from Cleveland, he was born in 1940. He graduated from the Metropolitan Community college and teaches music and the history or the Romany Holocaust at the University of Minnesota. His grandfather played bass with the John Brenkacs Gypsy Orchestra. Hancock's father is Hungarian Gypsy. The office of Presidential Appointments takes its recommendations directly from the various agencies it serves.

These Gypsies were not above discrimination. They faced it every day of their lives, and it is no different today. The persecution of Gypsies didn't start with Hitler; it was going on for hundreds of years before his reign. It didn't end with Hitler; it still goes on today, even in the United States. Today there are Romany Rights organizations that stand up to discrimination, try to get arcane laws taken off the books that are still in place, and try to assimilate the Romany people into society. While they are making progress, the Gypsies are far down on the list of humanity and equal rights. Gypsies are the world's minority, yet they have no minority rights. Worldwide discrimination and persecution still exist as exhibited by France in 2010 when they succeeded in repatriated Gypsies to Romania even though France was condemned internationally. Today the world only sees Black and White, and no one else counts.

Homestead Gypsies Circa 1915

Cards Courtesy of George Batyi

HOMESTEAD

Homestead is a small town less than three miles from Braddock. The Gypsies of this community settled there around the same time they did in Braddock. Early records show about twelve families living there. Throughout the years some of the Gypsies from these two communities intermingled on a regular basis. The funeral pictures that show a large group of Gypsies and musicians posing with an open casket is made up of Gypsies from both communities. There were many fine musicians who came from Homestead. By the 1930s, there were about fifty families living there.

Early documents show tension and separation between the two communities. The Gypsies of Homestead came from the same part of Hungary as the other Gypsies, but from the county of Zemplin. All the Gypsies of the other communities came from the county of Saros. (Zemplin and Saros were adjoining counties.) In a thesis written by Dr. Marchbin, in 1939, he said, "There are about forty Gypsy families living in Braddock. Other Gypsies who are more prosperous live in Homestead and McKeesport and are being assimilated principally into Slovak and Hungarian neighborhoods."

Julius Piskor, Erma Piskor on cimbalom (my grandmother), Gus Piskor, and Louis (Poodie) Krista

Front left on bass, Julius Piskor, back center Louis (Poodie) Krista, Front center, Gus Piskor and left, Butch
Photos property of the author

A few journals noted a difference in the Homestead Gypsies: one classified them as laborers and part-time musicians, and another said the Homestead Gypsies choose to work, while the Gypsies of Braddock refuse to work. My Uncle Gus Piskor was born in Cleveland, Ohio, in 1919. His family moved to Homestead when he was a young boy. When he returned home from military service in World War II, he joined the Homestead police force, where he worked for the next thirty years, retiring in 1978. He was also a violin player.

His first cousin Albert Piskor became a special agent for the FBI. He worked for the Bureau of Alcohol, Firearms, and Tobacco. He changed his name to Pryor to protect himself against any retaliation against his family from anyone he put behind bars. After he retired from the FBI, he taught criminology at the University of Pittsburgh. He was also a violin player and a violin dealer.

Journalists back then seemed to think that the only form of work for a Gypsy was manual labor. While this was a more stable form of work, playing music was the same as work. Some of the musicians played at the same places for years. There were three differences between the Homestead Gypsies and the Gypsies of the other communities. The first difference was the counties where they came from in Hungary. The second was that there were more Homestead Gypsies working than playing music. In the other communities, there were more Gypsies playing music than working. The third difference is in the last names. In Homestead last names were: Krista, Gorol, Ferry, Batyi, Miskovich, Kanolas, Martin, Tokar, and Piskor. In all the other communities, last names were: Ballog (Balog), Horvath, Ziga, Duna, Garber, Hallup, and Lacy (Lacey).

Homestead Gypsy Funeral, Circa 1940s

Homestead Gypsy Funeral, Butch in the Middle, Circa 1940s
Photos Property of the Author

Homestead and Braddock Gypsies; the young boy is George Batyi; from left, violin players: Cisko, Greenie, and Poodie.
George is about seven years old in this picture; he went on to become one of the best violinists among the Gypsies.
Photo Courtesy of George Batyi

Throughout the years there have been many marriages between the two communities, and a lot of the Gypsies from Saros County don't even know they have Zemplin blood. Today, for the most part, there is still separation between the communities. A few musicians have crossed the barrier. Louis (Poodie) Krista, a viola player, moved to Detroit and played with the great Gypsy violinist Jaroka Sandor. He also played with the well-known Gypsy cimbalom leader Gus Horvath and famous Gypsy violinist Ziggy Bela. Poodie's nephew George

Batyi is considered one of the best Gypsy violinists, and he frequently performs with the Gypsies from Chicago and Detroit. George's Uncle Butch was a well-known Gypsy violinist and was said to know more songs than anyone else. George still lives in Homestead and plays in the Pittsburgh area.

Homestead Gypsies, Circa 1920s

George Batyi Gypsy Orchestra, Homestead, Pennsylvania
Photo Courtesy of George Batyi

Only a few Gypsies still live in Homestead today, and most of them have given up the Gypsy life. While George has brothers that play violin, he's the only one who keeps the tradition going. By the end of the 1960s, all of the Gypsies moved out of Braddock. Most of them moved to Detroit where they continue the traditional Gypsy lifestyle and continue to play music.

Braddock is all but a memory now, and the Gypsies will never forget it. The city of Braddock and the Braddock Carnegie Library are putting together a history of the residents of Braddock. I will be contributing to the Gypsy section of that history.

Most of the Gypsies in this orchestra are from Braddock; a few are from the other communities.
Photo Courtesy of Tony Selepsky

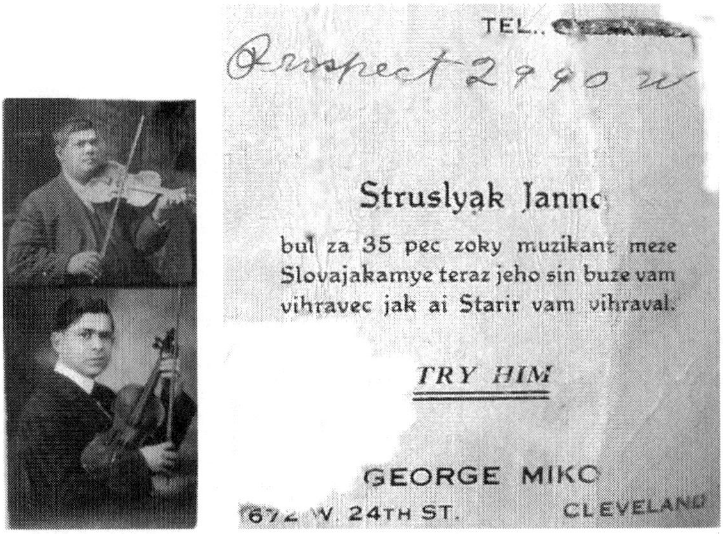

John Miko (Struslyak), My Great Grandfather, Circa 1915,
and His Son George (Fiki) Miko
Cards Courtesy of Elaine Horvath
From the Gus Horvath Collection

John Brenkacs, Circa 1910

CLEVELAND

The Miko and Lacy families were the first Gypsy families to settle in Cleveland in the mid-1880s. They moved to the Woodland and Buckeye area where a large community of Hungarians and Slovaks were living. The two Miko brothers would become an important part of the migration of the Hungarian Slovak Gypsies in America. These immigrants moved to the area because the only Slovak church in Cleveland was St. Ladislaus on Woodland (the third Slovak church in the country). The first Hungarian church in the United States was built in the same area a few years later in 1892.

Cleveland was the home of the fourth richest family in history, the Rockefellers, who owned the Standard Oil Company. John D. Rockefeller is listed as the richest man in history. His family's net worth as of 2008 is $318 billion. He died in 1937 and is buried in Cleveland's Lakeview Cemetery. Andrew Carnegie is listed as the second richest man in history; Bill Gates is number twenty.

The population of Cleveland was growing, and Cleveland remained in the top ten largest cities from 1900 to the 1960s. The Cleveland Hungarian population was also growing. In the 1920s throughout the 1950s Cleveland's Hungarian population was second to Budapest and was referred to as "the sister city to Budapest."

Music Is Life to Cleveland Gipsies

Violins and Cimbaloms Treasured by Romany Group

Hungarians Settled in Neighborhood on West Side

Eleanor Bandy, Tillie Duna, Lottie Duna, and John Brenkacs. The article talks about the Cleveland Gypsies defending their heritage, saying they are not the stereotypical fortune-telling,
traveling Gypsies.
Article Courtesy of the Cleveland State University,
Cleveland Press Collection

Alex Lehoczky and daughter Martha, who is a stenographer, Circa 1910
Photo Courtesy of the Cleveland Public Library
Cleveland Press Collection

In 1900 the population of Braddock was about 15,000 people compared to Cleveland's 400,000 people. One would think that all the publicity of the Gypsies of Braddock would be because of the small location and the small number of people, but that was not the case. The Gypsies of Cleveland were getting just about the same amount of publicity as those in Braddock, but in a much bigger city with about twenty-five times the number of people. The fascination with Gypsies was not limited to a location, for the same thing was happening in Detroit and Chicago.

This type of Gypsy had not been seen in America before, and for eighty years American journalists unwittingly documented their history.

By 1900 about forty Gypsy families had settled in the area of East 9th Street and Scovill Avenue, just a few blocks away from Cleveland's famous millionaire's row on Euclid Avenue. The two Miko brothers, John and Andrew, were the first of the Hungarian/Slovak Gypsies to arrive in America, and they are credited with helping other Hungarian Gypsy families come to America. They were successful business owners and musicians. They owned a tavern in the Woodland-Buckeye area. Then they sold the business and purchased multifamily homes in the area of Scovill Avenue.

The two Miko brothers married sisters Verona and Anna Lacy. The two sisters' brothers Stephen Lacy and John Lacy, and their sister Mary Lacy, who were all married, also lived in the area. Their father Michael Lacy, born in 1842, remarried and lived with the rest of the Lacy brothers and sisters, Alex, Margaret, and Rose. Michael Lacy died in 1905 and had over fifty grandchildren. This family would become one of the largest Gypsy families to date.

In the early years, there were many publications about the Gypsy musicians of Cleveland. Some of the most famous Hungarian Gypsy *primas* got their start there, such as Emery Deutsch, Ernie Kiraly, Joska Rabb, and John Brenkacs. There were more Hungarian restaurants and events in Cleveland than anywhere else in America. Cleveland also had the biggest Hungarian record label company in the country. Owned by Frank and Betty Zapponos, It was known as B&F Records; many of the Hungarian Gypsy orchestras made records under this label. The couple also operated the Hungarian radio station.

One of the most famous bands from this era was the John Brenkacs Gypsy Orchestra. In the 1920s they made eight records on the Columbia label and played all the major Hungarian events.

The orchestra consisted of John Brenkacs (lead violin), Rudolph Rigo (second violin), Albert Balog (viola), Geza Duna (bass), and Louis Ballog (cimbalom). (Louis (Bum) Ballog was my grandfather).

From left: a Hungarian friend Tony, George (bado-judi) Duna, Louis (Bum) Ballog, Geza (labud-do) Duna, Albert (ce-moon-ya) Balog, and Minor Richko
Photo Property of the Author

The John Brenkacs Gypsy Orchestra
From left: Albert Balog, Geza Duna, Louis (Bum) Ballog, Rudy Rigo, and John Brenkacs
Photographs Courtesy of the Cleveland Press Collection, Cleveland State University

In a book written in the early 1930s, the author, Walter Starkie, recounts a trip to Budapest in 1933 where he goes to the best restaurant in the city, The Marcus, where the King of the Gypsy violinists, Imre Magyari, was playing (p. 60). He said after he had talked to Magyari for some time, in between his intervals of playing, a tall, lean, dark-complexioned man came up to Magyari, put his arms around him, and kissed him on both cheeks. The man was Janos (John) Brenkacs, a Gypsy violinist who had returned to Budapest from Cleveland, Ohio, where he was the leader of a Gypsy Band.

Both Magyari and Brenkacs ordered bottles of wine, and the two Gypsies began to talk about old times while drinking wine. Every time Magyari played, Brenkacs took out his notebook and wrote down the name of the song. Brenkacs raised his glass and toasted Magyari saying, "Eljen, nobody is your equal, master." Imre Magyari bowed, and the men stood up and drank to one another. This toasting went on every few minutes throughout the evening until two o'clock in the morning. Imre Magyari was born in 1894 and died in 1940.

In 1934 the John Brenkacs Orchestra was called to Detroit for the opening of the Hungarian Village Restaurant, where they remained for almost two years.

Imre Magyari and His Gypsy Orchestra

John Brenkacs and His Second Wife Elizabeth in 1914

John Brenkacs and His Gypsy Orchestra, Louis (Bum) Ballog, and Geza Duna at the 1936–37 Great Lakes Exposition, World's Fair in Cleveland, Ohio.

Louis (Bum) Ballog and Mischa Bundy, Circa 1910
Bum talks about him and Mischa traveling to Braddock for a wedding where the Gypsies have been living for fifteen years.
Photograph Courtesy of the Cleveland Press Collection.

In 1936 the Great Depression was still going on. In an effort to boost the economy, the Great Lakes Exposition World's Fair opened in Cleveland, Ohio. The Exposition lasted two years and millions of people attended. The John Brenkacs Gypsy Orchestra was called back to Cleveland to play this event. They are pictured in the official souvenir guide. Other performers were Johnny Weismullur, the Three Stooges, Eddie Cantor, and many other stars. President Roosevelt, John D. Rockefeller, and Henry Ford all attended. After the World's Fair, Brenkacs moved back to Detroit. John Brenkacs was born in 1885 and died in 1964.

Other members of the John Brenkacs Orchestra: Rudy Rigo came from a family of violinists. He led many Gypsy orchestras. Rudy Rigo died in the 1960s.

Albert Balog (ci-mun-ya) was born in Hungary in 1898. He immigrated to the United States when he was a young man. He was considered one of the best musicians among the Gypsies. Albert Balog continued to play until his death in 1968.

Geza Duna (la-ba-do), born in 1896, played with many Gypsy orchestras and dance bands. He played his last performance at the Cleveland Hotel, where he died on stage in 1948.

Louis Ballog (Bum) was born in Hungary around 1890. He was considered one of the finest musicians among all of the Gypsies. In a book written in the 1930s, the author noted that Louis Ballog, a cimbalom player, taught many Gypsy musicians. He was also featured in many newspaper articles and is listed in a book about dulcimer-cimbalom players. His grandfather and father were also famous cimbalom players. Louis Ballog died in 1943.

Emery Deutsch was born in 1904. He grew up in Cleveland listening to the Gypsies play. He was a graduate of the Julliard School of Music. He wrote the famous songs, "When a Gypsy Makes His Violin Cry" and "Play Fiddle, Play." He composed over eighty songs. He was the musical director for a small radio station in Queens, N.Y. when the Columbia Broadcasting System took over. He continued as the music director, and the station became the center of CBS radio. While Deutsch was music director during the time that Benny Goodman, Andre

Kostelanetz, Bing Crosby, and many others signed on to CBS. After CBS he returned to Cleveland to play with the Gypsies. Emery Deutsch died in 1997.

Ernie Kiraly was born in 1921 and started studying the violin at the age of seven. He attended the Cleveland Institute of Music, Joseph Fuchs and violinist David Rubinoff were two of his teachers. He gave his first public recital at the Cleveland Hotel when he was fourteen. Later he started his career in Gypsy music. One of his most famous recordings was "Ernie Kiraly and his Hungarian Gypsy Orchestra." The band consisted of: Ernie Kiraly (violin), William Garber (tenor violin), Maxie Bandy (second violin), Carl Bandy (viola), Maxie Rigo (cimbalom), and Martzi Ballog (bass). The record was made in the 1950s and is still held in high regard. Ernie Kiraly (King) died in 1987.

Emery Deutsch

Joska (Joe) Rabb

From left: Maxie Bandy, Carl Bandy, Ernie (King) Kiraly, Maxie Rigo, Martze Ballog, and William Garber

Joska Rabb

Sandor Janos, Joska Rabb, and John Brenkacs at the Gypsy Cellar
Photographs Courtesy of the Cleveland Press Collection

Joska Rabb was born in Pennsylvania in 1916 and grew up in Cleveland. He taught himself to play the violin and furthered his studies at the Cleveland Institute of Music. Rabb said he took lessons from the "King of the Gypsy Violinists," John Brenkacs. Later he went to New York and studied with Maxie Fransko. After serving in World War II, he toured with Hungarian actress Ilona Massey. He returned to Cleveland, dressed in billowing sleeves and a purple cape, and started to play with the Gypsies of Cleveland. In 1955 he opened his own Hungarian restaurant, The Gypsy Cellar, on Buckeye Road. He became the main attraction and led an orchestra made up of Cleveland Gypsies. The Gypsy Cellar became a well-known spot for visiting celebrities such as Liberace and Zsa Zsa Gabor. Joseph Vogel, president of MGM studios, and Hollywood director Joe Pasternak were frequent visitors, which led to Rabb's cameo appearance in the 1962 movie *Jumbo*.

The restaurant closed in 1971, and Rabb briefly held positions in the mayoral administration of Ralph J. Perk and the Washington office of Ohio Senator William Saxbe. Joska (Joe) Rabb died in 1996.

Throughout the years many of the funerals of the Cleveland Gypsies were written about in the newspapers. In 1932, one headline read: "Gypsies Fiddle a Requiem for Uncle Lacy." The funeral was for John (Jan Ju) Lacy. Willie (yemetts) Horvath conducted the thirty-piece Gypsy orchestra playing the funeral dirge as the funeral procession walked to St. Martin's Church on Scovill Avenue. Before John Lacy's death, he was the bass player for Willie Horvath's Gypsy orchestra. During World War I, the orchestra played in Washington, appearing before President Wilson. Lacy was also a member of a Gypsy orchestra that performed in vaudeville houses all over America. He was survived by his wife, Fannie (funna) (Hallup), and nine children.

In 1933 Elsie Duna, ten, was playing in the schoolyard by the West Side Market when she ran behind a truck and was crushed to death. Willie Horvath's twenty-piece orchestra led the funeral procession. Dozens of Gypsy children carrying flowers flanked both sides of the white hearse as it made its way to St. Emerich's Church. A convertible sedan filled with flowers followed the hearse. Gypsies from all of the communities attended.

John Lacy (Jan Ju (yun-you) Funeral, Cleveland, October 9, 1931
Photographs Courtesy of the Cleveland Press Collection
Cleveland State University

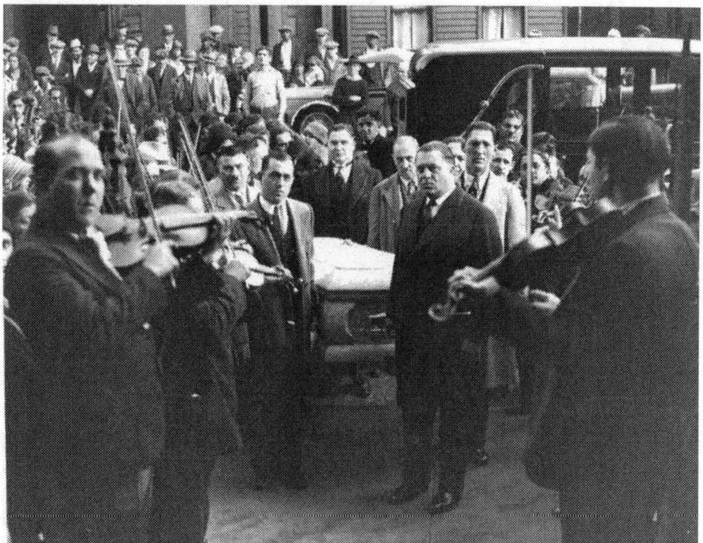

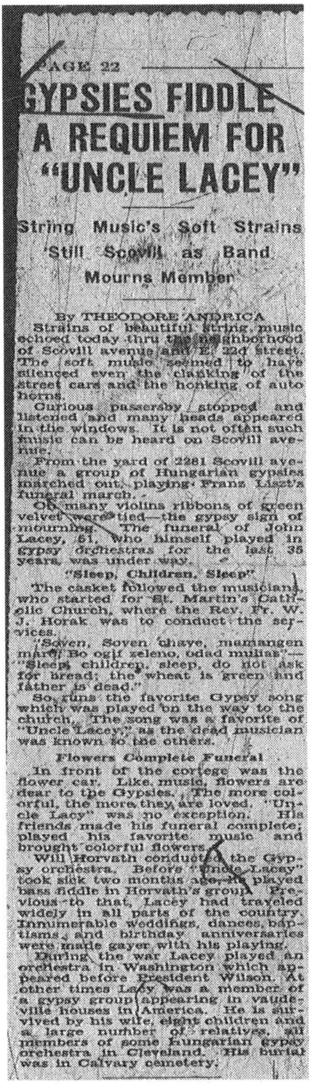

PAGE 22

GYPSIES FIDDLE A REQUIEM FOR "UNCLE LACEY"

String Music's Soft Strains Still Scovill as Band Mourns Member

By THEODORE ANDRICA

Strains of beautiful string music echoed today thru the neighborhood of Scovill avenue and E. 22d street. The soft music seemed to have silenced even the clanking of the street cars and the honking of auto horns.

Curious passersby stopped and listened and many heads appeared in the windows. It is not often such music can be heard on Scovill avenue.

From the yard of 2281 Scovill avenue a group of Hungarian gypsies marched out, playing Franz Liszt's funeral march.

On many violins ribbons of green velvet were tied—the gypsy sign of mourning. The funeral of John Lacey, 61, who himself played in gypsy orchestras for the last 35 years, was under way.

"Sleep, Children, Sleep"

The casket followed the musicians, who started for St. Martin's Catholic Church, where the Rev. Fr. W. J. Horak was to conduct the services.

"Soven, Soven chave, mamangen maro, Bo ogil zeleno, odad mulias"—"Sleep, children, sleep, do not ask for bread; the wheat is green and father is dead."

So runs the favorite Gypsy song which was played on the way to the church. The song was a favorite of "Uncle Lacey," as the dead musician was known to the others.

Flowers Complete Funeral

In front of the cortege was the flower car. Like music, flowers are dear to the Gypsies. The more colorful, the more they are loved. "Uncle Lacy" was no exception. His friends made his funeral complete; played his favorite music and brought colorful flowers.

Will Horvath conducted the Gypsy orchestra. Before "Uncle Lacey" took sick two months ago, he played bass fiddle in Horvath's group. Previous to that, Lacey had traveled widely in all parts of the country. Innumerable weddings, dances, baptisms, and birthday anniversaries were made gayer with his playing.

During the war Lacey played an orchestra in Washington which appeared before President Wilson. At other times Lacy was a member of a gypsy group appearing in vaudeville houses in America. He is survived by his wife, eight children and a large number of relatives, all members of some Hungarian gypsy orchestra in Cleveland. His burial was in Calvary cemetery.

John Lacy funeral 1931

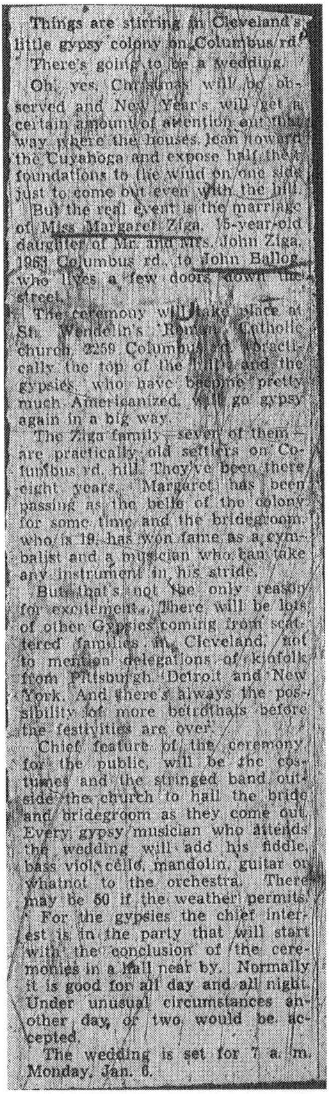

Things are stirring in Cleveland's little gypsy colony on Columbus rd. There's going to be a wedding.

Oh, yes, Christmas will be observed and New Year's will get a certain amount of attention out that way where the houses lean toward the Cuyahoga and expose half their foundations to the wind on one side just to come out even with the hill.

But the real event is the marriage of Miss Margaret Ziga, 15-year-old daughter of Mr. and Mrs. John Ziga, 1963 Columbus rd., to John Ballog, who lives a few doors down the street.

The ceremony will take place at St. Wendelin's Roman Catholic church, 2259 Columbus rd., practically the top of the hill, and the gypsies, who have become pretty much Americanized, will go gypsy again in a big way.

The Ziga family—seven of them—are practically old settlers on Columbus rd. hill. They've been there eight years. Margaret has been passing as the belle of the colony for some time and the bridegroom, who is 19, has won fame as a cymbalist and a musician who can take any instrument in his stride.

But that's not the only reason for excitement. There will be lots of other Gypsies coming from scattered families in Cleveland, not to mention delegations of kinfolk from Pittsburgh, Detroit and New York. And there's always the possibility of more betrothals before the festivities are over.

Chief feature of the ceremony for the public, will be the costumes and the stringed band outside the church to hail the bride and bridegroom as they come out. Every gypsy musician who attends the wedding will add his fiddle, bass viol, cello, mandolin, guitar or whatnot to the orchestra. There may be 50 if the weather permits.

For the gypsies the chief interest is in the party that will start with the conclusion of the ceremonies in a hall near by. Normally it is good for all day and all night. Under unusual circumstances another day or two would be accepted.

The wedding is set for 7 a. m. Monday, Jan. 6.

Marriage of Margaret Ziga to John Ballog, circa 1920s, Article courtesy Cleveland Press Collection, Cleveland State University

Elsie Duna (ten) Funeral 1933
Willie Horvath Leads the Gypsy Orchestra
You can see all of the young children carrying flowers as they walk on each side of the hearse. Photographs from the Cleveland Press Collection, Cleveland State University

John Ballog Funeral, July 16, 1971
Joska Rabb led the orchestra.
Photographs Courtesy of the Cleveland Press Collection, Cleveland State University

In 1942 Alex (Sandor) Lacy died. The famous Gypsy *primas* John Brenkacs led the funeral procession. Then Lacy's family moved to Chicago and became one of the largest Gypsy families in Chicago. His son Al (Shanko) Lacy became one of the most-respected Gypsies ever. Other children of Alex's were Achoo, Dave, Helen, and Sylvia.

In 1949 Gypsy musicians, led by John Brenkacs, played at the Gypsy funeral of Adam Birkas. Adam Birkas, lived with music and was buried with it. The Gypsies marched in front of the funeral car to St. Elizabeth's Church, playing the songs Birkas used to play.

In 1968 a newspaper headline read, "Gypsy Violins Cry Fiddler to Final Rest." The funeral was for Albert Balog. He was one of the best musicians among all of the Gypsies and played with all of the famous Gypsy orchestras, including the John Brenkacs Orchestra. The procession was led by primas Rudy Ziga; other primas were Joska Rabb, Al Margitza, and Frank Richko. Albert's son Rudolph (Rudy) Balog was also a famous Gypsy primas.

In 1971 another newspaper headline read, "Funeral for a Young Gypsy." Gypsy violinists played dirges, relatives and friends wept, and hundreds of Cleveland West siders watched as the coffin of John Ballog (age twenty-five) of 2619 Vestry was carried out of his house and loaded into the hearse for the funeral at St. Patrick church. Hungarian Gypsies from all of the communities were there as Joska Rabb led the orchestra.

PRESS AUG 9 '74

...PSY FAREWELL — The mournful and haunting music of Gypsy violins filled ... neighborhood around St. Patrick's Church, 3602 Bridge Ave., yesterday for ...s Shandor, 66, 1934 W. 44th St., who died Monday. Shandor was a well-...wn member of Cleveland's Gypsy community and musician at the old Gypsy ...ar Restaurant on Buckeye Rd. for 17 years. He was considered a master on the cymbalom, a Hungarian instrument something like a harpsichord and played with padded mallets. Following Gypsy custom, Shandor's relatives and friends came from Chicago, Detroit and New York for the wake and funeral and his fellow musicians gave him the traditional farewell in front of St. Patrick's. (Press photo by Tony Tomsic)

Julius Shandor Funeral.
Articles courtesy of Cleveland State University,
Cleveland Press Collection

PRESS SEP 25 '73

...LAY, GYPSY, PLAY — ...rank Richko, considered the elder statesman ...f gypsy violinists in ...leveland, was buried ...oday with the traditional pomp and circumstance of old Romany as ... band of gypsy musicians played their plaintive melodies from the ...olnar Funeral Home ...n Lorain Ave. to St. ...atrick Church on ...ridge Ave. Richko, who ...layed gypsy music here ...or nearly 40 years, died Friday at th age of 65.

(Press photo by Bernie Noble)

Frank Richko funeral.
Articles courtesy of Cleveland State University,
Cleveland Press Collection

Alex Lacy (Sandor) Funeral. In front: Shanko and Achoo's father.
October 26, 1942
Photographs Courtesy of the Cleveland Press Collection
Cleveland State University

Adam Birkas Funeral, February 16, 1949. John Brenkacs led the orchestra.
Photograph Courtesy of the Cleveland Press Collection
Cleveland State University

In 1974 the headline in the newspaper said, "Strings Weep a Gypsy Farewell." This funeral was for Casey Ziga. Primas Joska Rabb led an orchestra of thirty musicians. The article said, "Following an ancient custom, the group trailed behind the hearse, playing the 'Gypsy Farewell March,' over and over." Casey's son John Ziga would become one of the best Gypsy violinists.

There were many other Gypsy funerals featured in newspapers across the country that documented a tradition brought to the United States over one hundred years ago, and in Europe the tradition is hundreds of years old. In regards to a funeral in Chicago in 1950, an article stated: "Forty violinists play in the street for the funeral procession of Joseph Horvath, fifty-eight-year-old Gypsy musician. The musicians preceded the hearse to St. Michael's Church."

In Detroit a headline was, "Farewell to a Fiddler." The funeral was for one of the all-time Gypsy greats: Willie Horvath. Sixteen violinists marched before the hearse on the way to Holy Cross Catholic Church, playing music that was old when Brahms was born. One of his many American fans stood at his grave and said, "He played for my husband and me when we were courting." Then she said quietly, "We got married on his music."

Albert (ce-moon-ya) Balog Funeral, 1968
Rudy Ziga led the orchestra.

Casey Ziga Funeral, May 16, 1974. Rabb Joska led the orchestra.
Photographs Courtesy of the Cleveland Press Collection
Cleveland State University

Gypsy Violins Cry Fiddler to Final Rest

Albert Balog funeral 1968

Strings weep a gypsy farewell

By William F. Miller

Casey Ziga funeral 1972

The traditional Hungarian Gypsy funerals started in Europe hundreds of years ago and still continues in the traditional Gypsy style today here and abroad. Many of the most famous Gypsy primas funerals drew thousands of people and hundreds of musicians. The Hungarian/Slovak Gypsies of Europe played the same songs at a funeral that the American Gypsies played. The only song that was different was the funeral dirge, which was written by an American Hungarian Gypsy.

All the most famous Hungarian Gypsies in Europe were directly linked to the Gypsies in America. My mother and father were approved as a liaison between many of the Hungarian Gypsy orchestras that came to America by Zoltan Gombos who was the editor of the *Szabadsag,* the largest Hungarian newspaper in the U.S. He was a very powerful person. Presidents, governors, senators, and on down called upon him as a political advisor. The American Embassy would not allow these Gypsies to travel anywhere they wanted unattended; someone had to be approved to take responsibility for their safety and to make sure they didn't defect. Many of the Hungarian/Slovak Gypsies from Europe came to my house, including: Sandor Lakatos, Sandor Jaroka, Sandor Jaroka Jr., Buffo Rigo, Erno Kallai Kiss, Rinaldo Olah, and many more throughout the years.

****

Hungarian Gypsy funerals in Europe received a lot of attention especially when the number of mourners was in the thousands; then newspapers around the world had the story.

In 1956 in newspapers across the United States and all over the world printed the headline: "35,000 at Funeral of Gypsy

Musician." The funeral was for the famous Gypsy primas Sandor Bura; the funeral was in Budapest. Thousands of people lined the streets as the funeral procession of two hundred Gypsy musicians followed the hearse, playing a Gypsy dirge.

In 2007 Sandor Jaroka Jr. passed away in Budapest and thousands of people attended his funeral. Car after car was filled with flowers, followed by over one hundred Gypsy musicians with all of the most famous Gypsy musicians in attendance, including Boros Lajos and Roby Lakatos. The musicians marched while playing traditional funeral dirges, and a horse-drawn carriage carried the casket.

In 1984 Sandor Jaroka Sr., died, he was one of the most famous of the Gypsy primas. Thousands of people also attended his funeral, and hundreds of Gypsy musicians played. The famous one-hundred-piece Budapest Gypsy Symphony Orchestra was formed at this funeral.

My Mother and Father, Julius and Mitzi Piskor, and Sandor Lakatos and His Orchestra at my House on October 8, 1970
Photographs Property of the Author

Sandor Jaroka Sr., Sandor Buffo Rigo and Sandor Jaroka Jr. at My House on May 11, 1971

Today primas Sandor Buffo Rigo, who is married to Sandor Jaroka's daughter, is the president and musical director of the Budapest Gypsy Symphony Orchestra. In the early 1970s, Sandor Jaroka came to the United States on tour with his son Sandor Jaroka Jr., his son-in-law Sandor Buffo Rigo, and the famous clarinet player Erno Kallai Kiss. When they arrived in Cleveland, they came to our house, and my mother and father set up a table of food and drinks. Other Gypsies from Cleveland came to our house, and all of them played until the early morning hours. Sandor Jaroka went to Detroit where he stayed for a few months and was proclaimed "King of the Gypsies" after playing with the Gypsies of Detroit before going back to

Budapest. In a book written in 1993, the author interviewed Sandor Buffo Rigo, who said, "My wife's father, in my opinion, was the best Hungarian violinist. His name was Sandor Jaroka. He was crowned the King of the Rom violin by the Rom in Detroit, Cleveland, and Chicago."

One of the most famous and considered one of the best Gypsy primas was Sandor Lakatos, a descendent of the legendary Gypsy primas Janos Bihari. There is a long line of famous Gypsy violinists in the Lakatos family, including his son Deki Lakatos and a cousin named Roby Lakatos. In the early 1970s, Sandor Lakatos came to the United States on tour. When he arrived in Cleveland, he came to my house, and my mother and father made him and his orchestra a dinner of chicken paprikas and stuffed cabbage. Lakatos said he was a long way away for such a good home-cooked meal. Our Gypsy neighbors came over and played music, and Lakatos said he felt at home. Sandor Lakatos died in 1994 at the age of sixty-nine. About eight years ago, I met his son Deki Lakatos. When I told him who I was and that his father had come to my house, Deki said, "That was about 1971. My father talked about it." About three years ago, I met Roby Lakatos, and he said he knew of the Gypsies in Cleveland and Detroit and asked about Gus Horvath.

In the 1960s Kalman Banyak visited with the Gypsies of Cleveland. He went on to Las Vegas where he became the concertmaster for the Las Vegas symphony and recorded with Frank Sinatra. Banyak was born in 1923 and died in 1993. Even though the American and European Gypsies lived thousands of miles apart, they maintained a strong bond with each other as they did when they all lived together in Europe.

Cleveland

FUNERAL FOR THE BASS VIOLIN

Throughout the years, in Cleveland there was a Hungarian tradition for the funeral of the Bass Violin. The Hungarians call it *Bogo Temtes*. The symbolic mock funeral, held at the time of lent, ushered in the period of no music until Easter. Some of the articles that I found in newspapers start in the 1920s and go throughout the 1970s. In 1934 an article said that it was a centuries-old Hungarian custom. One of the Hungarians would dress as a clergyman and read the service from a mock bible. The Gypsy musicians would play traditional funeral dirges as the mourners wept. The fake clergyman brought down his hammer and shattered the instrument to bits. They used a bass violin because the strolling Gypsy musicians would put the money that was given to them at Hungarian festive occasions in the bass. The ceremony indicated that their source of revenue was lost to them until after Easter.

The Hungarian Ritual of "Burying the Bass Fiddle," Circa Mid-1930s
Men with feathered hats, from left: Joe Rigo, Louis (Bum) Ballog,
Louis Godla, Albert Gabor, Albert Balog, Andrew Gabor, and Rudi Rigo
Photo Courtesy of the Cleveland Press Collection
Cleveland State University

Burying the Bass, Circa Early 1940s
Seated: John Brenkacs; From Left: Frank Richko, Mary Lacy, Jerry Lacy,
Andy Balog, and Albert (ce-moon-ya) Balog
Photo Courtesy of the Cleveland Press Collection, Cleveland State University

In later years, Hungarian children would dress as Gypsies and stage the event. While the Gypsy orchestra played and mourners wept, the mock clergyman would pretend to break the bass. In Hungary, the tradition is not well known. It seems that it was only practiced in Cleveland. While no one wants to take credit for starting the tradition, many Hungarians claim the Gypsies who played in the Buckeye Road neighborhood probably started it. Throughout the years of this tradition, the Gypsy orchestras were hired to play these events. It seems unlikely that the Gypsy musicians would start a tradition that would put them out of work for six weeks.

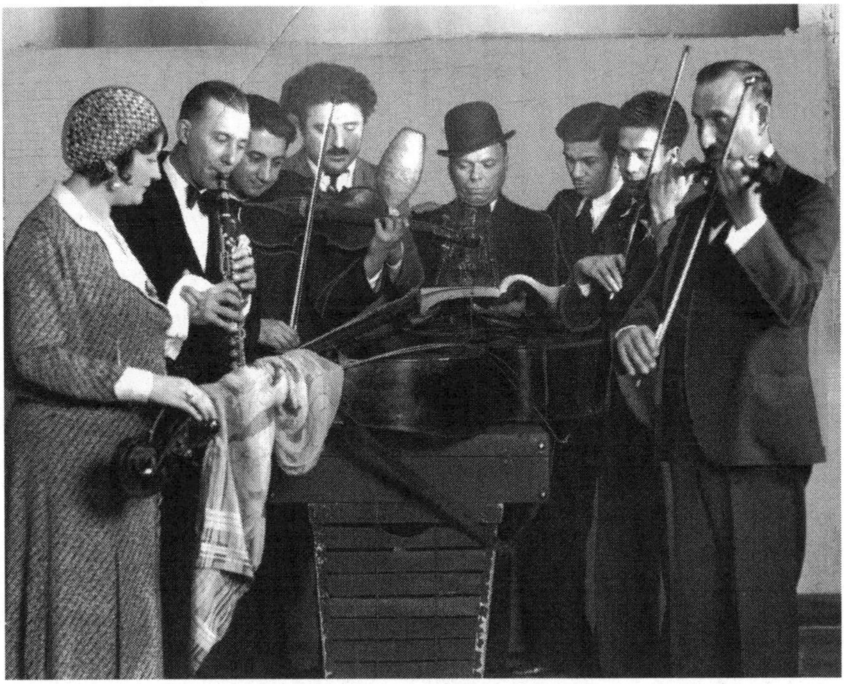

Burying the Bass, Circa 1940s
John Brenkacs Gypsy Orchestra
Photo Courtesy of the Cleveland Press Collection
Cleveland State University

Hungarian Tradition of Burying the Bass Fiddle, Circa 1930s
A mock clergyman reads from what looks like a phone directory; performed at the time of Lent.
Photo Courtesy of the Cleveland Press Collection
Cleveland Public Library

John Lacy (Jan Ju, pronounced yun-you) on bass, Rudy Miko on cimbalom, and John (Struslyak) Miko on violin Circa 1910

Bobby Richko and Raymond Lacy
Cleveland, Ohio

LOUIS CINA - VIOLINIST

Cleveland Night in Budapest

The Buckeye Road area of Cleveland had seven Hungarian churches and eight clubhouses, which held most of the community events. A typical calendar year of events at the churches and clubs consisted of twelve festivals, eleven New Year's Eve dances, fourteen picnics, twenty banquets, and over one hundred Hungarian weddings. Gypsy bands were a part of almost every one of those events. The Buckeye Road area had well over a dozen restaurants and taverns, not including the Hungarian clubs. The Cleveland Gypsies eventually settled in the Ohio City section of Cleveland's near west side. This area also had a large population of Hungarians as well as many Hungarian taverns, restaurants, and clubs. While most of the bigger restaurants had Gypsy orchestras playing on a regular basis, it was not uncommon to see a group of strolling Gypsy musicians, traveling between these taverns to play. Most of the Hungarian restaurants the Gypsies played in served the finest food and their cuisine was of the highest quality. The Gypsies not only played in Hungarian restaurants, but in many of the finest restaurants across the country. The combination of fine dining and Gypsy violins created an upscale, romantic atmosphere that made patrons feel important. The Gypsy musicians were well versed in music and could play any song in any genre. If someone requested a song they didn't know, they told the patron, "When you come back, ask for the song again." When the patron returned, they orchestra had learned the song and played it happily.

Cleveland Funeral, Circa 1930

George Richko Funeral 1968; From Left: Rudy Balog, Frank Kish, Adolph Ballog, Rudy Ziga, Dennis Ziga, and Casey Shandor

One of the most requested songs, other than "Fascination," was the "Anniversary Waltz." Many men would take their girlfriends to the most romantic restaurant they could find. What better place to "pop the question" than in an upscale, romantic restaurant with Gypsy violinists playing your girlfriend's favorite song? What's more romantic than taking your wife to a beautiful restaurant on your anniversary and dancing while the Gypsy orchestra plays the "Anniversary Waltz?" Many people hired Gypsy musicians for special occasions like weddings and private parties. People would often come back years later and say, "We got engaged to your music, married to your music, and now we're having our anniversary to your music."

Gypsy musicians not only played in Hungarian restaurants, they played in other ethnic restaurants and most of the large, famous restaurants and clubs that all likes of people went to.
By the 1930s Cleveland had the largest population of Hungarian Gypsies. The smaller communities of Gypsies in Uniontown, Johnstown, and Gary, Indiana, all moved to the larger communities of Braddock and Cleveland. While I found some reference to these Gypsies in newspapers, they were all advertisements of Gypsy musicians playing in restaurants. A 1931 Uniontown newspaper article stated that Andy Gabor of Penn Street died in the Uniontown Hospital from injuries received when he and four other members of the Uniontown Gypsy Band wrecked on McClelland Town Road. He was survived by his wife Susan and his children Mrs. Anna Balog of Braddock, Mrs. Mary Sartuci of Sharpsburg, and Helen, Pauline, and Andy Jr. at home.

Back row from Left: Georg (Feke) Miko, Geza Duna and not known
Front from Left: Bela (Bendy) Ballog, Archie Duna and not known
Photo Courtesy of Tony Selepsky

Chicago Gypsy concert 1960s, Albert Duna Primas, Billy Yedla cimbalom.

Early records of Youngstown, Ohio, show about twenty Gypsy families living in the area of Boardman Street. Some of the families that lived in Youngstown in 1910 now show up in the records as living in Cleveland in 1920. While some of the Gypsies continued to live in Youngstown throughout the 1930s, all of the Gypsies eventually moved to Cleveland. Youngstown produced some of the largest Gypsy families to date, such as the Balog's. The correct spelling is with one L, but some of the Gypsies changed it to Ballog to make it easier to identify Gypsies with the same first name. The Balog brothers George (poodla) and John (budaduck) and their three Balog sisters would become one of the largest families to date. Most of the history of this family has been lost, and their descendants don't know the history today.

Another large family from Youngstown started with the marriage of John Ziga (Chucklosh) and Mary Hollis (smyth-sun-ya). John had two children from a previous marriage, and Mary had four children from a previous marriage, and they had six or seven children together after they married. Other large Gypsy families from Youngstown were the Richko's, whose real name was Hricko, and the Bandy's, whose real name was Zurko.

Gypsy musicians came from every family in every community. Some became more famous than others, some played better than others, but all of them were great in their own respect. There are many other Gypsy families, some large and some small, one just as important as the other. The Gypsy primas would not be as famous without his orchestra. There are just too many to list them all.

****

There is a famous saying that sums up the Gypsy way of life" "The Hungarian wants only a glass of water and a Gypsy violin to make him drunk." Traditional music was a large part of the Gypsy lifestyle- socially and professionally. One social event began on August 4, 1927, when Cleveland's Hungarian Gypsies held their first picnic at the Malasky Farm on Short Road, off Broadview Road. Willie Horvath led the Gypsy orchestra of twelve musicians. The two cimbalom players, George Richko and Louis (Bum) Ballog, set up two cimbaloms back to back. Other musicians who played were Albert Balog, Rudy Rigo, and a young Ziggy Bela. The Gypsy women and the Hungarians dressed in traditional outfits. Goulash was the main dish, and over five hundred people attended. Newspaper reporters also covered the event.

First Cleveland Gypsy Picnic, 1927
Cimbaloms: George Richko and Louis (Bum) Ballog; Lead violin: Willie Horvath; Also Pictured: Albert Balog and a Young Ziggy Bela on Left

Emery Deutsch on Violin, Martze Ballog on Bass, and John Udvary on Cimbalom at Settlers Tavern Photographs Courtesy of the Cleveland Press Collection Cleveland Public Library

The ballroom at the Sheraton Cleveland Hotel held over one thousand people. Photographs Courtesy of the Hungarian Museum, Cleveland, Ohio

Boldy Garber performing a cimbalom solo; the back right bass player is Alex (bob-bay) Lacy; on the right second front, sitting, is a young Tony Ballog.

The 1950's became the strongest time for the Cleveland Gypsies. Almost one fifth of the population of Cleveland was Hungarian. For over forty years, there were at least two, most of the time three, Hungarian judges out of the nine serving on the bench of the Municipal Court of Cleveland. The chief of police as well as other high-ranking city officials were Hungarian. At one time, the mayor of Cleveland and the governor of Ohio were Hungarian. Every single one of them wanted Gypsy music, and the Gypsy musicians were in great demand.

In 1943 Jack Russell, who was Hungarian, was elected to city council and would become one of the most influential politicians in Cleveland's history. Within a few years, he was chosen by his fellow Democrats to serve as majority leader. In 1957 he was elected president of the Cleveland City Council, a position that held much power over the city. A half hour national television special was produced about his life, and

Russell even taught a course on practical politics at Harvard University. Jack Russell was also the biggest supporter of the Gypsy musicians; many of them were his personal friends.

In 1957 Jack Russell came up with the idea to hold a gala event that would honor famous Hungarians and would feature all of the famous Gypsy primas and musicians. Russell got the help of his friend, the famous Hollywood producer, Joe Pasternak, who was Hungarian-born and from Cleveland. Jack Russell named the event "Night in Budapest" after a famous restaurant on Buckeye Road. Joe Pasternak became the National Chairman of the event, and for the next fourteen years, it was Cleveland's biggest society event.

"Night in Budapest" Concerts, Cleveland, Ohio, 1957–1970
For fourteen years this was Cleveland's biggest society event. Throughout the years, thousands of people attended, including dignitaries, politicians, and movie stars.

All "Night in Budapest" Photographs Courtesy of the Hungarian Museum in Cleveland, Ohio

The first couple of years, the "Night in Budapest" concerts were held on Buckeye Road, but because of the huge demand for tickets to the event, it was moved downtown to the Sheraton Cleveland Hotel. Throughout the years Joe Pasternak brought many movie stars to the event such as: Zsa Zsa Gabor, Eddie Adams, Mitzi Gaynor, Jimmy Durante, Kurt Kasner, Bill Dana, Kay Stevens, Ilona Massey, Rudy Vallee, Paul Lucas, Tony Martin, Mary Ann Mobley, and many more. Joseph Vogal, president of MGM studios, attended the "Night in Budapest" concert every year and was honored in the 1961 event.

The average crowd topped one thousand people. Guests were greeted by a lineup of Hungarian men, dressed as Hussars. Their sabers were raised to form an arch for incoming guests. Two hundred women dressed in traditional outfits were the hostesses for the evening. Guests sat down to a dinner of the finest Hungarian food. Some of the finest opera stars, pianists, and comedians entertained the guests, but the highlight of the evening went to the Gypsy orchestra.

"Night in Budapest" Concerts in Cleveland, Ohio

Photographs Courtesy of the Hungarian Museum in Cleveland, Ohio

Every year the "Night in Budapest" concert featured a different primas.
Photographs Courtesy of the Hungarian Museum in Cleveland, Ohio

The night featured a full program of dancers, singers, and Gypsy musicians.

All of the most famous Gypsy musicians were there: violinists: John Brenkacs, Emery Deutsch, Joska Rabb, Erni King, Maxie Fransko, Rudy Balog, Frank Richko, Rudy Ziga, and Ziggy Bela; cimbalom: Gus Horvath, John Udvary, Alex Udvary, Albert Horvath, Maxie Rigo, and Boldy Garber; second violin: William Garber, Max Bandy, Carl Bandy, and Albert Balog; bass: Alex Lacy, Louis Lacy, Martze Ballog, Frank Horvath, Albert Ballog, William Hussar, and many others.

Many politicians attended the "Night in Budapest" concerts such as: Cleveland Mayors Ralph Locher and Carl Stokes; former Mayor Anthony Celebrezee, who went on to become the secretary of health, education, and welfare; and U.S. Senator Frank J. Lausche, who went on to become the governor of Ohio. In 1970, after fourteen years of the famous "Night in Budapest" concerts, Jack Russell retired, and the famous event ended.

In the 1930s groups of Gypsies began moving to Chicago and by the 1980s only a small group of Gypsies remained in Cleveland. The majority of them moved to the cities of Detroit, Chicago, and Las Vegas. Today about forty families remain in Cleveland, with only a few musicians left, and none of them play traditional Gypsy music. To date, Cleveland is the longest-running community of Hungarian Gypsies. There have been Hungarian Gypsies living there for over 120 years.

Sandor Janos, Martze Ballog, and Alex Udvary
at Settler's Tavern on Buckeye Road

Jimmy Ginna on Violin
Photographs Courtesy of the Cleveland Press Collection

FIERY HUNGARIAN GYPSY MUSIC pours from the strings of instruments played by John Ziga, 16, of 3018 Bridge Ave. (left); Alex Udvary, 12, of 1923 W. 44th St., and Louis Lacey Jr., 16, of 1923 W. 44th St. Alex plays the cimbalom.

PRESS MAR 30 '60

Youths Keep W. 44th St. Gay With Hungarian Gypsy Music

By STEPHANIE MACKAY

When teen-age boys gather for a musical jam session at 1923 W. 44th St., it's not with drums and horns.

Instead, playing violins, bass and cimbalom, the boys recreate the fiery, gay or melancholy music that inspired their ancestors centuries ago.

These teen-agers have an unusual and rich musical heritage — that of the Hungarian gypsy.

"You can't do justice to the music unless you feel it — and you have to be a gypsy to feel it," explained Alex Udvary, 12, already an accomplished cimbalom player.

Louis Lacey Jr., 16, added, "There are several groups of musicians in our crowd, and each one plays a different type of music — popular, Latin or jazz. But they all play Hungarian gypsy music."

Alex, Louis and John Ziga, 16, of 3018 Bridge Ave. often play music together at the Lacey and Uduary home on W. 44th St. They have performed for special occasions both in their neighborhood and in other parts of the city. They'll play tomorrow night at West Side Community House, 3000 Bridge Ave.

Play by Ear at Early Age

But each plays with other groups among the approximately 20 gypsy teen-agers in the neighborhood.

"The problem with our crowd is they're all pianists," said Louis, whose bass always is in great demand. "The older boys, 18 and over, have similar trouble—they all play violin."

Although the young musicians study music with professional instructors, most have played violin or piano by ear from early childhood. A few may play the clarinet, the only non-string instrument among traditional gypsy bands.

Sons of musicians, they frequently pick up the instruments their fathers play. Alex's father, John, has played the cimbalom, a popular gypsy and Hungarian instrument, at the Gypsy Cellar and other night spots.

Louis is following the footsteps of his father, bass player at the Theatrical Grill.

"We'd go to parties where our fathers and other men played and watch them," says Alex. "Then, from records, we'd learn the melodies."

Play for Weddings and Funerals

Weddings and funerals always bring together gypsy musicians, the boys say. Relatives from Detroit, Chicago and New York will gather for the event. Frequently the young men and boys will play, too.

During a gypsy funeral, the favorite songs of the deceased are played, as well as a traditional funeral march. The musicians, carrying large bass viols and cellos as well as violins, play in the street as they follow the pallbearers from the funeral parlor to the church.

Music is the most important part of the Hungarian gypsy's life, the boys say.

"We're not traveling gypsies or fortune-tellers," they stressed. "In summer the gypsies travel to other cities to find jobs playing in night clubs and resorts. But we have only one home."

Johnny Ziga, Alex Udvary, and Louis Lacy, 1960
In this article, sixty years after some of the other Hungarian/Slovak Gypsy articles, they still have to defend themselves as not being fortune-telling Gypsies.
Article Courtesy of the Cleveland Public Library
Cleveland Press Collection

GYPSY WOMEN

Throughout this book there has been much written about the Gypsy men, but we can't overlook the Gypsy women. Back in my grandfather's days, the Gypsy women were known by the man's name. For instance, my grandfather's real name was Louis Ballog; the Gypsies called him "Bum," and they called his wife, "Bummeinya." Her real name was Margaret (Lacy). My great-grandfather's real name was John Miko; the Gypsies called him "Struslyak," and they called his wife "Struslyakinya." Her real name was Anna (Lacy). Other names were Plata, whose wife was called Platinya; Silly, whose wife was called Sillinya; Budaduck, whose wife was called Budaduckinya; and there were many more.

This only happened in the early days with the Gypsies who came directly from Europe. As time passed and the Gypsies became more Americanized, the tradition stopped. While some of the Gypsies still have nicknames, the women only go by the last name of the man.

Many of the families were large. My grandmother came from a family of nine children, and she had eleven children. Her sister had fourteen children, and my grandfather's sister had twelve children. The Gypsy women were very much like other women of the era: they had to know how to cook and be resourceful. My grandfather was always playing music and making money, and by the time his youngest child was born, his oldest children were having children of their own. With eleven children and three grandchildren, there was never enough money.

In the early days, school was important. The Gypsies in America wanted their children to learn to read and write and to learn the American ways, something that was much harder to achieve in Kassa. Their skills were already destined, so that was the extent of their education.

Divorce was rare among these early Gypsies. If the man died, the woman would remarry, since the man was the source of income. These women were the backbone of the family, they kept everything in order and together. These Gypsy women were well respected and still talked about today.

When the men went to play, they dressed in traditional Gypsy outfits. Some wore head scarves and earrings; some wore the traditional Gypsy vest. Many men still dress this way when they go to play. At some of the events the men played, the women dressed in traditional outfits, and the entire audience would admire their beauty while news reporters would flock to photograph them.

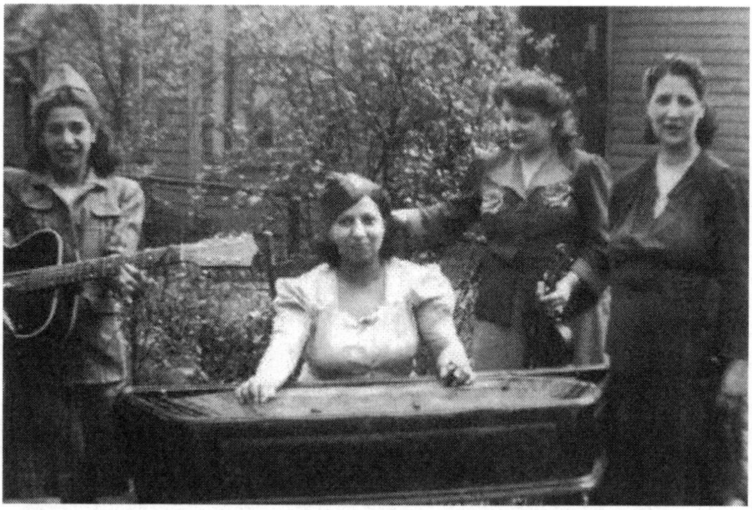

Gypsy Women from Left: Geza Duna, Eleanor Kish, Tillie Horvath, and Mary Richko (bobina)

Gypsy Women, Circa 1930

Left Photograph: Emma Miko (vieu) and Margaret Ballog (bum-mein-ya)
Right Photograph: Mary Ziga (smyth-sunya) and John Ziga (chucklosh)

Anna Lacy Mary Ballog Phillypineya and Platinya

THE GYPSY COUNTESS VERONA

Many of the Gypsy women were musically talented, such as Verona Miko and Mary Ballog. One of the most famous of these Gypsies was Verona Miko, born in Hungary in 1887. Her father was Andrew, and her mother was Veronica Lacy. A child prodigy on the cimbalom, she started learning the instrument at the age of six. By the age of thirteen, she was already performing, displaying the skills of a master. She also played the violin, piano, and cello. Within a few years, she went on tour in Europe, often performing for royalty. When she returned to the United States, she went on the road with a vaudeville troupe. She headlined in all the famous vaudeville theaters from New York to California. I found dozens of newspaper advertisements of her playing in these theaters across the country. She headlined in one of New York's famous vaudeville shows, which was

billed as "The Big Show" at the famous Hippodrome theatre. Most of the famous stars of the era performed at the Hippodrome.

Elsie Bandy
Sixteen years old

Margaret Balog
my grandfather's sister

Verona Miko
cimbalom virtuoso

Photographs Courtesy of the Cleveland Press Collection at Cleveland State University

From left back row: Maxine Richko, Rosie (Rumba) Horvath, Bootsie Richko
front left row: Sylvia Udvary and Rosaday Richko

Braddock Gypsy girls. left: Marion Horvath

Chicago Gypsy Girls Going to a Party

While in Milwaukee performing with a Hungarian symphony orchestra, she met the Count Dean Szechy de Szechy Falva of Budapest. Verona was a very beautiful woman, and the count fell in love. Although they were married, the count's family did not approve of the marriage and disowned him, cutting him out of everything, including the fortune. The count did not care; he went to Cleveland with Verona and entered into a business career.

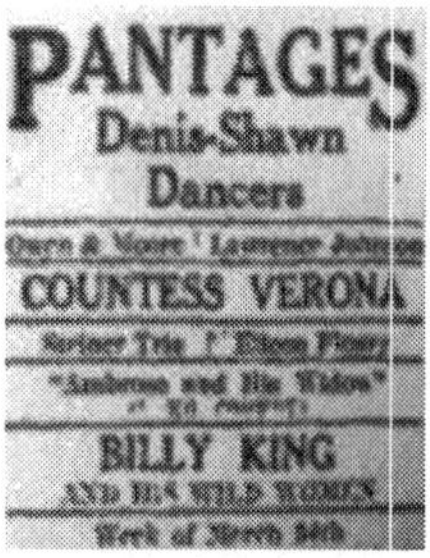

Verona began working under the name Countess Verona Szechy. It's unclear what happened to the marriage. She later remarried to Carl Robbins, a publisher; she remained married to him for the rest of her short life. She still held the title of countess and was billed as the "Gypsy Countess Verona."

In 1916 she recorded two records under the Columbia label and wrote the song "Gypsy Rag." The song is listed in the book of Ragtime music and was recently recorded by Nora Hulse on her CD of women in ragtime music billed as "sixty years of Ragtime piano." Verona also performed with the Cleveland Symphony Orchestra several times.

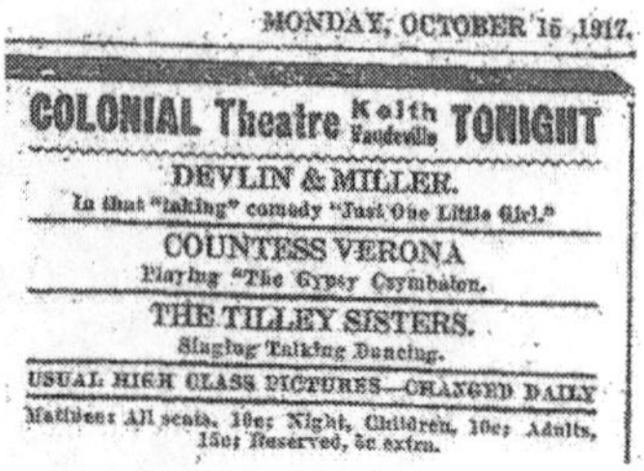
MONDAY, OCTOBER 15, 1917.

COLONIAL Theatre Keith Vaudeville TONIGHT

DEVLIN & MILLER.
In that "talking" comedy "Just One Little Girl."

COUNTESS VERONA
Playing "The Gypsy Cymbalon.

THE TILLEY SISTERS.
Singing Talking Dancing.

USUAL HIGH CLASS PICTURES—CHANGED DAILY

Matinee: All seats, 10c; Night, Children, 10c; Adults, 15c; Reserved, 5c extra.

In 1933 she played with the Cleveland Symphony Orchestra under Conductor Arthur Rodzinski, along with the famous Hungarian violinist Joseph Szigeti, performing the Hary Janos suite(the first time played by the Cleveland Symphony). Verona died in 1937 at the age of fifty.

"Gypsy Rag" Written by the Gypsy Countess Verona in 1916

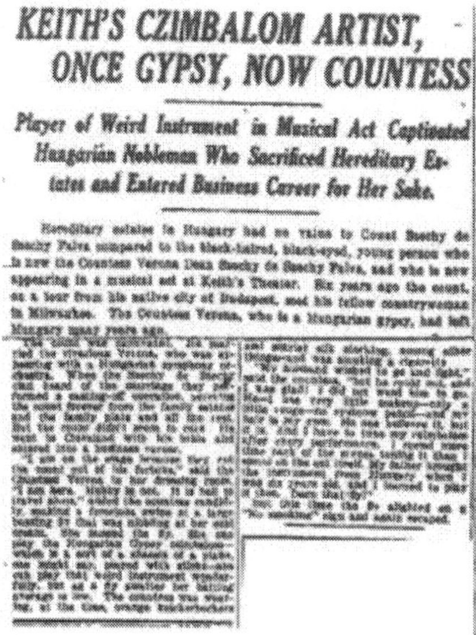

KEITH'S CZIMBALOM ARTIST, ONCE GYPSY, NOW COUNTESS

Player of Weird Instrument in Musical Act Captivated Hungarian Nobleman Who Sacrificed Hereditary Estates and Entered Business Career for Her Sake.

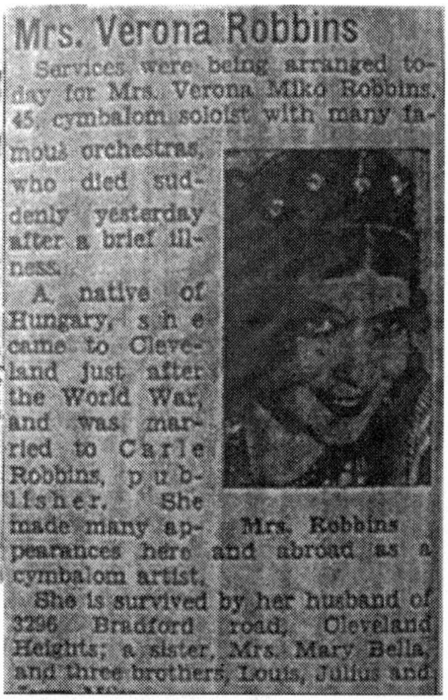

Mrs. Verona Robbins

Services were being arranged today for Mrs. Verona Miko Robbins, 45, cymbalom soloist with many famous orchestras, who died suddenly yesterday after a brief illness.

A native of Hungary, she came to Cleveland just after the World War, and was married to Carle Robbins, publisher. She made many appearances here and abroad as a cymbalom artist.

She is survived by her husband of 3296 Bradford road, Cleveland Heights; a sister, Mrs. Mary Bella, and three brothers, Louis, Julius and

Mrs. Robbins

The Gypsy Countess Verona
One of the Most Famous Among all the Gypsies

Photographs Courtesy of the Cleveland Press Collection and the Cleveland Symphony Orchestra

Detroit Gypsies Rehearsing for a Concert

Ziggy Bela Orchestra, Hungarian Village, Detroit
Photograph Courtesy of the Gus Horvath Collection

DETROIT

In the early 1920s, the first of the Hungarian Gypsies showed up in the Detroit, Michigan, area of Delray. The Gypsies of Homestead were the first of these communities to settle in Delray. Around the same time in Europe, articles in newspapers across the country were reporting, "Negro Jazz Artist and Gypsy Musicians at War in Hungary." The articles were about jazz music that was becoming popular in Europe and the jazz bands from the United States that were playing in Budapest. The Gypsy musicians felt threatened and said that the music was erotic and crazy. Several towns in Hungary agreed with the Gypsies, and the Hungarians said jazz had to go. The Hungarians and the Gypsies of Budapest were not ready for a change in music.

In 1924 in the United States, in an effort to preserve old-time music from being taken over by jazz, Henry Ford formed the "Henry Ford's Old-Fashioned Dance Orchestra." Ford loved the violin, and when he was alone in his office, he often played one of the violins from his collection, including his $75,000, 1703 Stradivarius. One of the songs he played was "Turkey in the Straw," but he never learned to play well. He often sponsored fiddle and square dance competitions in an attempt to get the young ones back into the old-time music and dancing—and away from jazz.

The orchestra consisted of a violin, a sousaphone (tuba) or bass fiddle, a dulcimer, and a cimbalom. Musicians came from all over the country to audition. Many famous musicians auditioned and drew national attention in newspapers around the world. The cimbalom player was a Gypsy from Braddock by the name of William Hallup; the Gypsies called him "Skinny." Henry Ford had a special cimbalom made for Hallup. The orchestra was under a strict contract with Ford and was not allowed to perform anywhere unless approved by him. They made records, toured the country, and played at all of Henry Ford's big functions.

Many dignitaries attended those functions, including the president and other elected officials, movie stars, and Thomas Edison. Ford worked for Thomas Edison before he started his car company and the two remained friends until Edison's death. Ford was the one who asked Edison's son to catch his father's last breath in a vial; it is in the Ford Museum today. By 1926 the orchestra's fame was almost gone, and Ford used the orchestra to sell his new line of cars in 1926 and 1927 in a national radio broadcast. The orchestra changed throughout the years, but William Hallup continued to play.

Henry Ford's Old-Fashioned Dance Band
Henry Ford's Seventieth Birthday, July 30, 1933
From Left: Henry Ford, William Hallup, Maurice Castel, Clayton Perry, and Edwin Baxter
From the Collections of The Henry Ford

William Hallup
"Skinny"

Homestead/Detroit Gypsy Band
standing violin player to Mike Funti and Joe Ferry on cimbalom, bass Joe Kanalos, sitting violin player Andy Piskor, and sax player Joe Kanalos jr.
Photo Courtesy of Julius Piskor (not my brother)

Juilus Rakoczi funeral 1957, Delaray, MI

In 1947 Henry Ford died and the orchestra was over. William Hallup's cimbalom is in the Ford Museum with Henry Ford's Stradivarius. Hallup died in the 1960s.

Hallup was among the first of the Gypsies of Braddock to move to Detroit. In a publication in the 1930s, the author conducted a door-to-door count of the Gypsies in Delray. The adults numbered 163: 83 males and 80 females. This count was made up of Gypsies who had moved to Detroit from Braddock and Homestead. The Gypsies cite the reason for moving to Detroit was the demand for Hungarian Gypsy music.

The 1930s article in *The American Journal of Sociology* about the Gypsies of Delray states, "The adult musicians are the teachers: Rudi Miskovic teaches the bass, Louis Ballog teaches the cimbalom, and Willy Horvath teaches the violin. The older Gypsy boys who take lessons from these teachers, teach the younger boys, such as Rudy Kanalos, who is just fourteen, teaches Andy Piskor."

In the 1930's the Hungarian population of Detroit was growing as well as the Gypsy population. Hungarian restaurants and clubs were opening, such as the Hungarian Village. Gypsy music was in demand. Detroit was a continuance of the Braddock Gypsies; many of the young Gypsy musicians from Braddock were now adult Gypsies in Detroit. This new era of Gypsies in Detroit would go on to produce some of the finest Gypsy musicians, and a few of them would reach the level of national fame.

Ziggy Bela concerts

One of these musicians was the great Gypsy primas Ziggy Bela. Born in Braddock in 1910, Ziggy's real name was Julius Margitza. He came from a long line of talented Gypsy musicians. The famous Billy Garber, who died in 1935, was his uncle; so playing violin came easy to him. At ten years of age, he was giving recitals and at sixteen he had his own orchestra. He quickly became famous in Detroit and became one of the most recognized Gypsy violinists in the country. In the 1950's Ziggy started his famous Gypsy Picnic Concert.

Within a few years, the concerts were attracting national attention and hundreds of people were attending the event to see as many as fifty to sixty Gypsy musicians led by Ziggy Bela, under the musical direction of Gus Horvath. Ziggy invited musicians from all of the communities to play. The Gypsy Picnics went on for over twenty years and became one of Detroit's best-known events.

The last concert for the late George Ballog of Detroit. The tribute was given in the streets before players marched with the coffin, which was on its way home to Braddock, Pennsylvania. October 28, 1948

Ziggy recorded two albums, *Dreams of Budapest* and *Czardas*. Ziggy Bela died in 1989, and even today people still ask about him.

Gus Horvath was born in Braddock in 1916. He began studying cimbalom with Louis (Bum) Ballog; he furthered his studies in New York with the great cimbalom player Zsiga Bela. Horvath's cimbalom skills were among the best, and he was known throughout America, Canada, and Europe. Gus made many recordings and performed in many of the finest places. In 1948 he purchased a cimbalom from Hungary and flamboyantly embellished it himself; that cimbalom became an attraction in itself. Horvath died in 2001, and his cimbalom is displayed in the Michigan State University Museum.

Arthur (Artie) Rakoczi was born in Braddock in 1930. He was one of the most loved Gypsy violinists. Artie played in many of the finest places and was known throughout the country. At the age of six, he could already play Hungarian Rhapsodies on the violin and he also played piano. He also worked under the name, Artie Nelson. While all of these Gypsies had stories to tell, I like this one: In 1948, Artie was playing in a fine Hungarian restaurant in Detroit when in walked the famous movie star Bela Lugosi, who was Hungarian. Lugosi had just finished the movie *Abbott and Costello Meet Frankenstein*. It was his last time that he played Dracula in the movies.

Artie, being mischievous, thought he would have some fun. He knew his sister Dorothy and her friends, Edna and Mitzi (my mother), were at his house with other friends; they were all about sixteen years old. He called his sister and told her that a famous movie star had just walked in; he instructed her to bring the girls to come and see him. He would not tell them who it was. He told Lugosi what he had planned, and when the girls walked in, Bela Lugosi went into his Dracula character. The girls were scared and would not even go near him. Lugosi assured them that he would not bite, kissed their hands, and began to sing in Hungarian while Artie played. The girls weren't taking any chances, so they left. Arthur Rakoczi made three records and died in 1977.

Gus Horvath Cimbalom in the Michigan State University Museum

Gus Horvath Gypsy Orchestra

Left: Album Recorded in 1963 *Right: Arthur Rakoczi*

Back Left: Emma Lacy; Front from Left: Dorothy Rakoczi, Mitzi Piskor, Edna Shandor, Maggie, Bob Nelson; Sitting: Fannie Hallup

From Left: Jay Kalleo, Arthur Rackoczi, Bobby Garber, Billy Garber, Rudy, Don Andre; Center: Gary Selepsky on Cimbalom
Photo Courtesy of Tony Selepsky

Delray 1972
Photo Property of the Author

Artie Nelson aka Arthur Rakoczi

Rudy Chicko, Artie Nelson and Billy Rose

Billy Rose was born in Braddock in 1931. His father taught him to play guitar when he was ten years old and singing came naturally. Billy made several records and played in top-rate venues. Many movie stars made a point to watch him perform. In 1948 the famous actor Anthony Quinn took Rose to a recording studio where he made a record of Quinn's favorite songs—just for him. Rose's family name is Slepsky; he comes from a family of Gypsy musicians. His sons, Chris, Anthony, Gary, and Ryan, are all famous musicians in Detroit. Billy Rose became an icon and still plays in the Detroit area.

Bob Nelson Gypsy Orchestra

Early Ziggy Bela Gypsy Orchestra

There are many famous families from Detroit who all come from a long line of excellent Gypsy musicians. The Shandors (Skeeter, Darin, Kevin, David, and Vincent) are all top-notch musicians. Jimmy and Steven Shandor from Cleveland perform all over the country, and Julius Shandor was a famous cimbalom player. There are the Garbers: Frank and Boldy were great cimbalom players; Billy Garber Jr. was considered among the best; Albert and Bunker were well-known; and Kevin Garber is a headliner. And the Chicos (Rudy, Eddie, and Billy) are all great musicians and Don De Andre, a talented pianist, preformed with many of the top entertainers and headlined in Las Vegas.

In the early 1970s, after Sandor Jaroka left Cleveland, he went to Detroit, where he lived for a few months, playing at the Hungarian Village with the Detroit Gypsies. Jaroka became close friends with the Gypsies of Cleveland, Detroit, and Chicago. Also in the early 1970s in Cleveland, I went to see a

Romanian Gypsy group that was on tour from Europe. The cimbalom player was Toni Iordache, who is considered the best cimbalom player ever. Many tributes are made to him every year, and Gypsy orchestras have paid tribute to him on a record. After he left Cleveland, he went to Detroit where he went to see the Detroit Gypsies play. He stayed with them, playing and drinking until the early morning hours. Toni Iordache was born in 1942 and died in 1987.

Julio Bella (Margitza)

Django Reinhardt and Stéphane Grappelli

Julius Margitza was born in Braddock in 1934 and started playing the violin at the age of five. In the early 1960s, he recorded the album *The Hot Jazz Violin*. His recording name was Julio Bella. Other members of the Hot Club Band were: Billy Margitza (piano), Andy Hullup (bass), Billy Kallao (drums), and Marty Kallao (guitar). The album was mentioned in a book about Django Reinhardt and is listed on the Eddie South and Stuff Smith websites. A cut from the record is on various artists' records, including Reinhardt and Grappelli, Eddie South, Stuff

Smith, Joe Venuti, John Figro, and others. All of them knew the Gypsies well. John (ya-low-low) Ziga from Chicago also became a well-known jazz violinist and close friends with Eddie South. Julio Bella died in 1988.

In 1946 the famous Gypsy guitarist Django Reinhardt toured America for his first and only time with the Duke Ellington Orchestra. Their first stop in America was Cleveland, Ohio. The Gypsies went to meet Django, who wanted to stay among the Gypsies in Cleveland, but his schedule with Duke Ellington was tight, and he didn't have time. Django invited them to New York where he said he was planning to stay for a while. After he left Cleveland, he travelled to Detroit and went to the Hungarian Village. Ziggy Bela and his Gypsy orchestra were playing there. Ziggy quickly called for his son Julio, who was only about twelve years old and already playing Reinhardt's music. Julio played for Django, who was impressed with how well Julio played; Django predicted a bright future for Julio. Django's last stop on the tour was Chicago, where he recorded with Ellington. The Gypsies of Chicago met Django, among them was John (ya-low-low) Ziga, and they played for him. In New York, Django stayed in the Hampshire House and played at the Café Society Uptown. Django got to know Maxie Fransko and often showed up where Zsiga Bela and my grandfather Gus Piskor were playing. Throughout Django Reinhardt's stay in America, he got to know the Hungarian Gypsies of America well.

Ziggy Bela Gypsy Picnic Concert

Detroit Gypsy Concert
Rudy Fransko and Gus Horvath

Eddie South knew the Gypsies of Cleveland, Detroit, and Chicago very well; they recorded with him. His famous record *Black Gypsy* got its name from him being friends with the Hungarian Gypsies. When he was with them, he called himself a "black Gypsy." Stuff Smith also knew the Gypsies well. And when Joe Venuti came to Cleveland for a week, I went to see him every night with a large group of Gypsies. We would end up drinking and playing in his hotel room. I also got a chance to meet Gypsy guitarist Berelli Lagrene, who said we were the first Gypsies he met in the United States. We took pictures of each other.

There are many different types of Gypsies; their language, traditions, and lifestyles are all different, but they all have music in common. The Gypsies of Spain have Flamenco music, played by the likes of the Gypsy Kings. I met the Gypsy Kings in Cleveland, and while our dialect was not the same, some of the Gypsy words are universal among all the different types of Gypsies, and they knew what type of Gypsy I was. The same goes for the Gypsies of France. Django Reinhardt was the first jazz musician in Europe. He took jazz and incorporated it with French music and Blues and started what was termed as "Django Gypsy Music." His father played the cimbalom, so Reinhardt knew Hungarian Gypsy music. When I met Berelli Lagrene, our dialects were different, and both of our dialects were different from the Gypsy Kings. Berelli said his grandmother came from the same Gypsies that I come from; she was born in Kassa, Hungary. Guitarist Larry Coryell and drummer Billy Cobham were also there. When Billy Cobham saw us, he said, "I know what Gypsies you are; you're the violin players."

I have met different types of Gypsies from all over the world, and the dialect closest to or the same as mine comes from the Gypsies of Hungary and Slovakia. When I met Roby Lakatos, I said to him, "We don't speak the language well." He said, "Neither do we."

Detroit Gypsy Orchestra

Ziggy Bela Funeral 1989
Photo by the Author

Julius Shandor Gypsy Orchestra
Photos Courtesy of the Gus Horvath Collection

Detroit Funeral

Other Gypsies in the United States were mostly associated with fortune telling. The Hungarian Gypsies wanted nothing to do with that, and there was very little contact between the two groups. Both dialects were different from each other and so were the lifestyles. Both groups of Gypsies knew of each other and some knew each other personally. All the different types of Roma-Gypsies were segregated from each other and did not socialize with each other, marriage between the groups was rare and while the Gadje discriminated against all Gypsies, these different groups of Roma-Gypsies discriminated against each other which made it hard to organize for representation. Today some of the so called Romani Rights Activist will not represent all Gypsies.

At some point in time, hundreds of years ago, it's evident that all the different types of Gypsies were all one. Society had a lot to do with the stereotypical traveling, wandering Gypsies. Everywhere they went, they were thrown out, forcing them to wander because of their lifestyle. One article in the newspaper said, "The Gypsies were thrown out of the city because they were knocking on doors, asking for water." I don't make excuses for the Gypsies' behavior, but when you're refused water, does one have to ask why.

Some of the states had laws that were just repealed within the last ten years that allowed anyone to enter a Gypsy's house at any time to inspect it. I was recently at Cleveland State University doing some research, when I ran into an author who I had met a few years earlier. He overheard me talking to the librarian about Gypsies and said, "There was no reason to write about Gypsies unless they were doing something wrong." I quickly showed him some articles I had with me that proved Gypsies weren't doing anything wrong. In this day and age when it is illegal to discriminate against others, his thinking, like most *gadje* (non-Gypsies), is that Gypsies can do no good.

Today in Detroit, the young Gypsy musicians play jazz, make records, and play in many of the finest jazz clubs and festivals throughout Michigan. While there are many Hungarian Gypsies still living in the Detroit area, there are only a handful who can play traditional Hungarian Gypsy music.

From Left: Albert Ballog, Dennis Ziga, and Fred Ballog

Willie Horvath on Violin, Martze Ballog on Bass, and Billy Garber on Second Violin

GYPSY GUITAR AND VIOILN

There were many Gypsies who had fine musical instruments; some had old Italian violins, French and Italian basses, and the best Gibson guitars. There were two musical instruments owned by Gypsies that stand out from everyone else's, and they are known all over the world.

In the early 1960s, Gypsy violinist Arpad D'Zurko went into a violin shop in San Francisco and found an old, Italian violin in excellent condition. It was labeled Antonius Stradivarius Cremonensis, 1734. While most violins with similar labels are fake, D'Zurko was convinced by the tone and other identifying features that he had found the "real deal." He named the violin the "Gypsy Stradivarius." Violinmaker Frank Passa challenged him on the authenticity of the instrument and talked him into getting an expert appraisal. D'Zurko sent the violin to New York to one of the worlds' leading violin experts: Rembert Wurlitzer. Wurlitzer had the exact dimensions of the mold used by the

Stradivarius family, and D'Zurko's violin fit perfectly. Wurlitzer said, "The matter of the mold is interesting, but incidental to the actual authentication of the violin." Wurlitzer pronounced the violin to be the true handiwork of Francesco Stradivarius, son of Antonius.

In 1949 Gypsy guitarist Lefty Shevak of New York asked one of the greatest guitar makers of all time to make him a guitar. John D'Angelico, whose shop was located in New York, was considered the best maker of archtop guitars. He made 1,164 guitars in his lifetime. D'Angelico made one of the most famous guitars in history, the "Teardrop" archtop guitar, which is in the Smithsonian Institute. The guitar's worth has been estimated at one million dollars, and experts say it could go for more at auction. Lefty Shevak's guitar was made on August 31, 1949. Listed in D'Angelico's ledger as a "New Yorker-Left cutaway, serial number 1826, made for Lefty Shevak." At some point Lefty decided to sell the guitar.

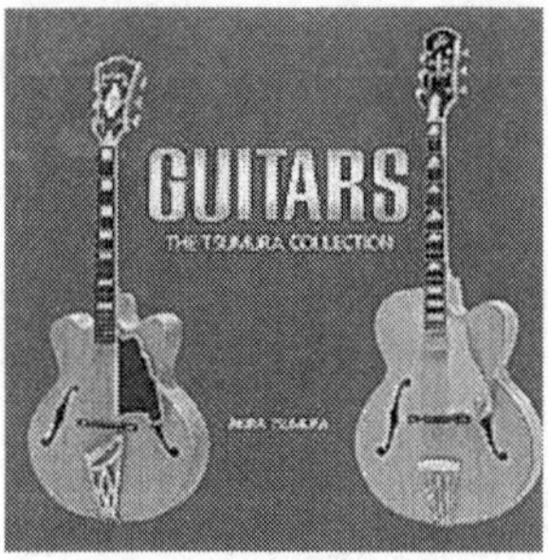

Lefty took it back to John D'Angelico and asked him to convert it into a double cutaway. The only one who worked for D'Angelico at the time was his apprentice, James D'Aquisto, who became another icon of archtop guitar makers. They converted the guitar into a double cutaway, and Lefty sold the guitar to his Gypsy cousin Smokey D'Zurko in Chicago.

Smokey had the guitar for a few years until it was stolen. D'Angelico guitars are rare, and individual guitars are easily identified. It was found in the possession of Pete Townsend, the guitarist for the Who. When Townsend was informed about the guitar, he quickly gave it back to Smokey. When Smokey passed away, his wife sold the guitar to the famous guitar collector, Akira Tsumura. Akiro's famous book *Tsumura Guitars* has a picture of the guitar on the cover. Inside the book, the caption under the pictures of the guitar reads: "D'Angelico New Yorker, old-style headstock, #1826, originally left-handed and converted to a double cutaway, once owned by Pete Townsend."

NOTABLE GYPSY MUSICIANS

Gypsy music was an important part of life to the Gypsies. While there were many Gypsy musicians who played traditional Hungarian Gypsy music, there were many Gypsy musicians who ventured out of the traditional genre.

Alex Kallao was born in Braddock, Pennsylvania. Blind at birth, he began his musical career at the age of three. A child prodigy, Alex began studying seriously with the renowned pianist and conductor Julius Chajas. Already critically acclaimed, Alex gave his first recital at seventeen. Alex moved to New York where he quickly started playing the jazz music he loved at New York's finest jazz clubs, such as the Blue Note and the Embers. Alex played opposite and toured with many famous stars: Ella Fitzgerald, Dizzy Gillespie, Oscar Peterson, Gene Krupa, Buddy Rich, and many others. His debut at Carnegie Hall was opposite the Count Basie Orchestra. Alex appeared on the *Tonight Show* with

Steve Allen three times. He recorded many acclaimed albums and has appeared with the Detroit, Toronto, and Buffalo symphonies. Alex currently lives in San Francisco and continues to play jazz. His brothers Marty & Bill are famous Musicians.

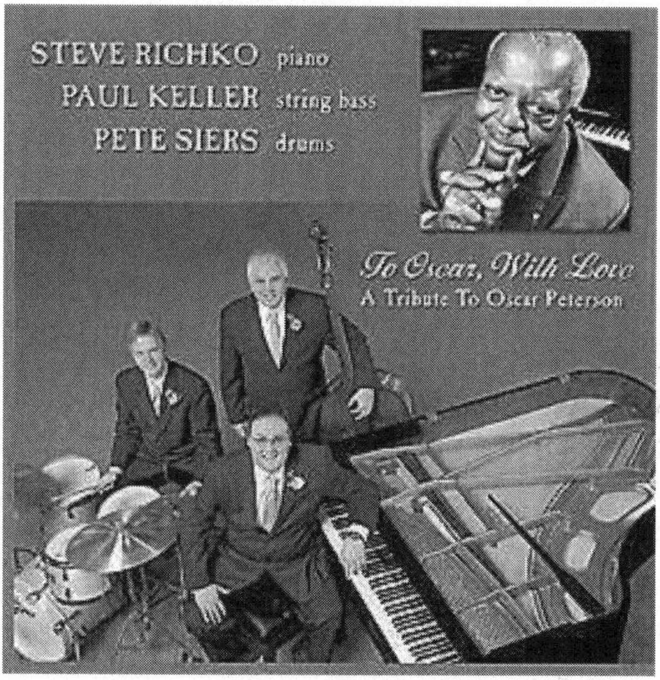

Steve Richko

Steve Richko was a great talent who was just becoming acknowledged for his exceptional virtuoso piano skills when he suddenly passed away in 2010, leaving Gypsies and the Jazz world in shock. A child prodigy, by the age of 12 he was already playing in the style of his favorite pianist Oscar Peterson, in his twenties his name was soaring with the best in jazz and his talent was compared to the best. He will be missed by many, and he left a legacy that will never be forgotten. His grandfather was Primas Frank Richko.

Rick Margitza

Rick Margitza was born in Detroit in 1961. He comes from a long line of Gypsy musicians, and his father played in the Detroit Symphony Orchestra. He started at the early age of four, playing piano, violin, and oboe, before he switched to tenor

saxophone in high school. He attended Wayne State University, Berkley, the University of Miami, and Loyola University in New Orleans, where he lived and played for four years. Rick graduated with a bachelor's degree. He toured with Maynard Ferguson, Flora Purim, and Airto before moving to New York in 1988. Margitza played and recorded three albums with Miles Davis and performed with Miles at the Monterey Jazz Festival. Margitza has recorded and played with many jazz artists such as: Chick Corea, Eddie Gomez, Bobby Hutcherson, Tony Williams, and Maria Schnieder, but there are too many to list them all. He played with Dave Douglas on his Grammy-nominated album at the Grammy Awards. Margitza has recorded eleven albums of his own and is listed on the discography with eighty-one sessions, an amazing accomplishment since some other big-name stars only have a fraction of this total. Margitza made a dedication to me on his CD, *Bohemia*. He currently lives in Paris, France.

Louis Kish was born in Cleveland, Ohio, in 1943. He started playing bass at an early age. In the 1960s, he began playing with the "King of Polka," Frankie Yankovic. He toured the country with Yankovic and headlined in Las Vegas.

Yankovic had his own TV show called *The Yankovic Hour*; later the shows' name was changed to *Polka Varieties*. Louis Kish was the bassist on the weekly television show. Kish made many records with Yankovic and other polka bands. Kish is on the famous recording "All Stars of Polka" under the name, Lou Bashell. The last name in Gypsy means "to play a musical instrument." Yankovic went on to win the first Grammy given for Polka music, and he sold more than thirty million records.

Julius Piskor Jr. was born in Cleveland in 1951. He started studying piano at eight years old. By thirteen he had formed his own band called Jr. and the Hi-Boys. Under his leadership, the band quickly started playing professionally.

The other members of the band were Fred Ballog (Freddy boy), Hiram Rivera, and José Ortiz, and they were all about the same age. By the age of sixteen, Jr. landed the group a gig at one of Cleveland's biggest clubs. Leo's Casino started out as a jazz club and hosted all the jazz greats: Charlie Parker, Miles Davis, Ella Fitzgerald, Oscar Peterson, Dizzy Gillespie, and everyone else. With the start of Motown, the club quickly became an R&B club and hosted all the great R&B stars: Stevie Wonder, Smokey Robinson, Marvin Gaye, Ray Charles, The Supremes, and many more. The club's audience was racially mixed, and Dick Gregory called the place "the most fully integrated nightclub in America." While the Hi-Boys played all the pop music of the era, their favorite group was Sly and the Family Stone. On one of the three occasions they performed at Leo's Casino, they played the night before Sly and the Family Stone were scheduled to play. Sly had heard about the band everyone was talking about, and he and his band showed up the night Jr. and the Hi-Boys played. Sly said he never heard four white guys play with so much soul, and he was amazed by how well they played his music. They were offered to tour Europe with the Motown group "The Donations" and other Motown stars, but at sixteen years old, all the parents said no.

When the Gypsies heard of the success Jr. was having with the band, a wave of Gypsy bands followed suit, and Julius Piskor Jr. led the way for the Gypsies to enter a new era of music.

Dakota Horvath started singing at the age of two. By the age of five, he was singing professionally. Dakota's grandfather Albert (Stacks) Balough was considered among the best Gypsy musicians. Dakota's idol is Frank Sinatra, whom he met in 1994. Dakota's singing in the style of Sinatra caught the world's attention. He has appeared on many TV shows such as *Live with Regis and Kelly, Entertainment Tonight, Maury Povich, Good Morning America, The Jerry Springer Show, The Rosie O'Donnell Show, The Queen Latifah Show,* and many more. He was in two movies: *Street Corner Justice* and *Silent Hunter*. He has performed with Tony Bennett, Natalie Cole, Don Rickles, Howie Mandell, Herbie Hancock, Rick Springfield, and too many more to list them all. He made world headlines when he performed at the Brad Pitt/Jennifer Aniston wedding and at the *Sopranos* Emmy Award HBO party. He did all of that by the time he was sixteen. Today Dakota performs throughout the country and in Las Vegas.

Dakota Horvath

Justin Shandor was born in 1989. At twelve years old, his mother introduced him to the music of Elvis Presley. He instantly connected with Elvis, and his music has been a part of Justin's life ever since. He performs all over the world.

Justin has won the Midwest and Las Vegas Elvis Impersonator contests and was hailed "best new tribute artist" by Elvis Tribute Artist Radio. Justin comes from a

long line of famous Gypsy musicians on both his mother's and his father's side. Justin tours with the "Elvis Birthday Bash" as young Elvis. He also is a fine musician and plays piano. Today Justin Shandor lives in Las Vegas where he headlines and performs in the *Legends* show and at the Elvis museum.
Justin has become one of the foremost Elvis impersonators in the world.

While a lot of Gypsies played other types of music, most of them could still play traditional Gypsy music, speak the language, and continue the Gypsy heritage, but the exceptions are the young ones of today.

WEDDINGS AND CHRISTENINGS

It didn't take much for the musicians to get together to play. They played at their own parties, christenings, birthdays, or just got together and played for fun, but there was one organized event that was a sight to see. The traditions of a Gypsy wedding started in Hungary/Slovakia long before the Gypsies arrived in America. Many of the eastern European countries followed the same tradition. In the early days, here's how it went. The couple announced they wanted to marry (in the older customs, it was prearranged), but it would not become official until they picked a *starosta* (sta-rosta), who was generally an older man. He would be a very important part of the wedding, from the engagement to the end of the reception. At the reception the starosta would serve as the master of ceremonies, acting on behalf of the groom. The bride would pick a *swadka* (swad-ka), who would act on her behalf. The swadka often purchased the cake for the wedding. (Starosta and swadka are Slovak terms.)

Wedding of Julius Piskor Jr. and Susan Ballog
Cleveland, Ohio

Wedding of Donald Lacy and Patty Ballog
Chicago, Illinois

Wedding of Ron Polo and Fifi Lacy
Chicago 1961

Photographs Property of the Author

The engagement ceremony would take place at the home of the girl's parents or because of a large family it would be held in a hall, most of the time this was a planned event, there were occasions where it happened as a surprise at a party that was already in progress. Then the oldest person at the party would do the ceremony and the starosta was picked later. The starosta would take the couple to be married and tie their hands together. In his speech, he would wish them a happy, long marriage; the best of health, happiness, and prosperity; many healthy children; and so forth. He would then say: "Engaged to be married is the future Mr. and Mrs. so and so," and that made it official. After the ceremony the traditional wedding would be planned for a later date. Today the engagement ceremony and the "Tying of the Hands" are gone. I can't remember the last time this ceremony was done, but every other part of the traditional wedding is intact. Everyone knows the phrase "tying the knot;" it came from this tradition. Many nationalities believe the "tying of the hands" ritual is the actual wedding ceremony and the traditional wedding is just a formality.

On the morning of the wedding, family, friends, musicians, and the wedding party would gather at the bride's house. The musicians would play festive music in the fashion of a *czardas* while the bride was getting ready. They kept the tradition of the groom not seeing the bride until it was time to say the vows, so the groom would not be there. When it came time to go to the church, everyone would wait outside, except for the wedding party. The musicians would continue to play as the wedding party came out of the house two at a time. Bridesmaids and ushers would stop at the top of the porch steps and then proceed to their cars. The last one to come out of the house was the bride, who was welcomed by a round of applause.

Barbara Lacy and Father Al (Shanko) Lacy
Chicago 1957
Some of the musicians are Louis Ballog, Ray Duna, and Brothers John and Kalman Duna

Photographs Property of the Author

Miniature Bride – Phyllis Greenie
Chicago 1961

Jeanie Bunzik 1957
Stepfather Albert Baker
Violinists Duke and Rudy Rigo
Photographs Property of the Author

At the church the musicians would often play all of the music required at the service, or they would accompany the organist provided by the church. As the service ended, the musicians would play as the bride and groom exited the church.

The reception would be a formal event, some held in modest halls, some going to the extreme of huge receptions. The Gypsies went through all of the formalities of a wedding reception, but what made it different from a *gadjo* (non-Gypsy) wedding was the large Gypsy orchestra.

At the dinner, the starosta would make a speech for the purpose of collecting money for the bride and groom. He would start the collection off with a donation of his own, then go to every table, passing a bowl or basket so that everyone could put money in it.

For the bridal dance, the Gypsies followed the Slovak custom of the *redovy*, which the Hungarians also followed. The Redovy is the name of the bridal dance and the custom. The musicians played the traditional *redovy* song. There are many recordings of this song on the Internet. While no one knows the exact words, there are over one hundred different verses written for it. I picked two examples that fit these Gypsies.

> "Play musicians, play for me.
> Play musicians, play for me.
> On my happy wedding day.
> On my happy wedding day."

> "Put some money in the plate.
> Put some money in the plate.
> Let the whole family help out.
> Let the whole family help out."

As the musicians played the *redovy* song, the guests would line up to dance with the bride. The starosta would be in charge, making sure everyone got a chance to dance with the bride. Guests would give money to dance with the bride, and the swadka would collect the money, sometimes pinning it on the bride. Then she would serve the guests a piece of cake. When the *redovy* was over, the party started. The Gypsy musicians would play to have a good time. The men and women would form circles, holding each other's arms around the waist. Some circles would be large, sometimes with two or three going at the same time, dancing and singing as the orchestra played Gypsy music. The Gypsy wedding lasted for two days. The first day was formal, and the second day was more relaxed, hosted in a smaller hall with catering, drinks, and Gypsy music.

****

Another Gypsy tradition that goes back as far as one can remember is the baptism of a baby. No one knows when, how, or why the tradition started. These Gypsies come from the Catholic denomination, and many are faithful churchgoers, as were their ancestors in Hungary. They follow the traditional ritual of the Catholic baptism. They pick godparents and baptize the child one month after birth. They don't wait longer for fear the baby would not be protected against evil. After the baptism ceremony, the parents bring the baby home. They place the infant under a table, usually the dining room or kitchen table, and they say the words, "I took you out a Jew and brought you back a Catholic." And that makes the baptism final. A newspaper article from around 1930 said that at a baby's christening party, the parents would place a violin bow in a male child's hand and toast to the baby as a future Gypsy primas.

Today some of the Gypsies still continue these traditions, although some of the rituals are based more on superstition. Superstitions fall under the category of folklore, old wives tales, and urban legends. For example, the idea that it's bad luck to walk under a ladder, break a mirror, or step on a crack, or that Friday the thirteenth and black cats are ominous. Saint Gregory I "the Great" ordered people to say "God Bless You" when someone sneezed in order to prevent the spread of disease. *Yakenda,* also known as the evil eye, and many more were universal among all people. Some superstitions verge on the level of the occult and witchcraft; however, these Gypsies never went that far or took part in any such practice.

HIS DESTINY IS ASSURED

Raymond Duna (left) is only a month old but he is destined to become a gypsy violinist. Last night a celebration was held at his parents' home, Mr. and Mrs. Geza Duna of 1879 W. 22d street, inconnection with Raymond's christening. One of the important parts of the feast was the placing of a violin bow in Raymond's hand. This act will insure Raymond's becoming a good violinist, according to the Hungarian Gypsy tradition. Over 100 Hungarian gypsies from Cleveland, Akron and Youngstown attended the party. Photo at right shows Lottie Duna of 1885 W. 22d street and Frank Ricko of 2515 Jay avenue, godmother and godfather to Raymond.

Gypsy Christening for Raymond Duna, Early 1930s
The godparents, Frank Richko and Lottie Duna (who married each other at a later date), placed a violin bow in Raymond's hand. According to Hungarian Gypsy custom, this would ensure that Raymond would become a good violinist.
Article Courtesy of the Cleveland Press Collection, Cleveland State University

MORE NOTABLE GYPSY MUSICIANS

Alex Udvary was born in 1948 in Cleveland, Ohio. He started playing piano at the Cleveland Institute of Music and learned to play the cimbalom from his father, John Udvary. Alex is considered the best cimbalom player in America and is also known throughout Europe. He has performed numerous times with symphonies across the country and has recorded with Eugene Ormandy, conducting the Philadelphia Orchestra. He was musical director for the Hungarian Theatre and Dance Company in Cleveland. He has had a television special and given numerous lectures about the cimbalom. Loran Maazel and Janos Kiss have written pieces for the cimbalom especially for Alex. He has arranged, composed music, and written the words to the "Vikings Fight Song" for Cleveland State University. He has recorded with Beki Lasslo and the Hungarian State Folk Ensemble, and he has more than a

dozen recordings to his credit. Alex currently lives and performs in Chicago and frequently tours the country.

Tony Ballog was born in Cleveland. He started playing violin at the age of seven. With his family's musical background, he was destined to become one of the best Gypsy violinists ever. Tony attended the University of Miami and studied with George Zozoftsky and Louis Krasner. He has won many violin competitions and performed with the Miami and Las Vegas symphonies. At twelve years old, he was featured in the famous "Night in Budapest" concerts in Cleveland. He also was featured in the Midwest Folk Festival and has become a favorite across the United States and Europe. He currently performs in Chicago with Alfonso Ponticelli and Swing Gitan, playing in the fashion of Stéphane Grappelli and Django Reinhardt. Tony has made several records.

John Ziga was born in Cleveland in 1944. He started learning the violin at the age of four. He studied with the

renowned violinist Josef Gingold, who was known as the "second greatest teacher" of his time. Gingold was concertmaster for the Cleveland Orchestra and taught Joshua Bell and many other symphony violinists. Ziga went on to study at The Juilliard School under Dorothy DeLay; she preferred to be called Miss Delay. Miss DeLay was considered the "greatest teacher" of her time. Many publications were written about her. Some of her other students were: Itzhak Perlman, Cho-Liang Lin, Mark Kaplan, and many more concert violinists. John Ziga performed and recorded with the Dalton Boys, playing bass, and he played violin with José Feliciano. He has appeared on the *Tonight Show* with Johnny Carson and *The Merv Griffin Show*. John Ziga has made many recordings and comes from a long line of famous Gypsy musicians. Today he is considered among the best Gypsy violinists ever. Currently he lives in the Detroit area, where he continues to perform in many of the finest places.

George Batyi was born in Homestead, Pennsylvania, in 1959. He started learning the violin at the age of five. George was the youngest of his brothers and sisters and grew up in a house where his three brothers, father, both grandfathers, and several uncles played daily. He was playing with them by the time he was seven years old. At ten years old, he was accepted in the Chatham College Music Institute and studied under Jack Goldman of the Pittsburgh Symphony Orchestra. At twelve years old he played at the Pittsburgh Folk Festival, and at sixteen he had his own Gypsy orchestra. George has been featured in many folk festivals across the country. He toured Slovakia with the group Slajane. He has performed at the Hungarian picnic at Kennywood Park for the last fifteen years. George has made many recordings and is

considered among the best Gypsy violinists ever. George lives in Homestead and performs at the Gypsy Café in Pittsburgh.

Frank Richko was born in Buffalo, New York, in 1908. His father was Louis, and his mother was Julia Fransko. Frank moved to Cleveland when he was a young man. He studied under Nicholas Zabu, the Hungarian violinist, and with Charles A. Reychlik. He performed with the George "Spike" Hamilton Orchestra (whose son is the famous actor George Hamilton). He was one of the lead primas at the "Night in Budapest" concerts in Cleveland. Frank Richko was a well-known Gypsy violinist, and he made several recordings. Frank died in 1973.

Rudolph (Rudy) Balog was born in Cleveland in 1922. He started playing the violin at the age of seven. With two of the best Gypsy teachers among all the Gypsies—his father Albert (ci-moon-ya) and his Uncle Louis (Bum) Ballog—teaching him to play, he was destined to become a great violinist. Balog furthered his studies professionally. He was one of the lead violinists in the "Night in Budapest" concerts and was a well-known Gypsy violinist who played in the finest places. Rudy said, "For over one hundred years, before World War I, a Balog has played in one of the three cafés in Kassa, Hungary." Rudy died in 1999.

Rudy Ziga was born in Youngstown, Ohio, in 1917. He began learning violin at an early age. His family moved to

Cleveland when he was a young boy. Rudy came from a long line of Gypsy musicians, so his ability to play came naturally. He furthered his studies with a student teacher of Joseph Gingold and became a favorite in the Cleveland area. It is said that his tone on the violin was that of the greatest Gypsy violinist, Imre Magyari, and that no one could play a better *halgato* than him. Rudy became a well-known violinist in the Cleveland area. Rudy Ziga died in 1998.

Martze Ballog was born in Gary, Indiana, in 1924. He moved to Braddock, Pennsylvania, when he was a small child. Martze began playing at an early age, too. While Martze was not a prodigy, it was discovered early on that he had a special ability to play. At the time, he didn't know he had the rare gift of "absolute ear," more commonly referred to as "perfect pitch." With perfect pitch you can tell the key that a doorbell or a car horn is in. You automatically can tell the key of any song and in a group of musicians, he could not only pick out which instrument was out of tune, but also pick the string that needed to be tuned and whether it needed to be tuned higher or lower. He moved to Cleveland and used this rare gift to his advantage. He studied with some of the best Gypsy musicians, such as Louis (Bum) Ballog and Willie (Yemmets) Horvath. He furthered his studies professionally and learned to read music. He made many records, played with Jaroka Sandor, and

was well known. Martze played bass, but he was capable of playing any instrument. Martze died in 1999.

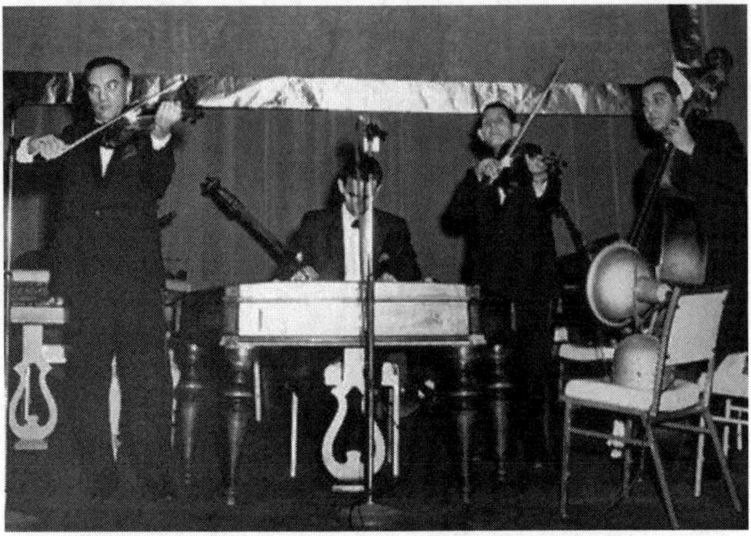

Bela Barath, Alex Udvary, Gaza Varga, and Martze Ballog

Ernie King, Dennis Ziga, Max Bandy, Rudy Ziga, Martze Ballog, and Alex Udvary

JENNY MOORE

While Gypsies were doing great with music, there were other Gypsies doing great things, such as, Jenny Moore and her mother Angela (Piskor) who is my sister. Jenny was diagnosed with Leukemia at the age of two. Her mother, Angie was so obsessed with the thought of losing her child that she figured the only way of saving her was to find a cure. Within a few years Jenny was also diagnosed with Thyroid cancer. Now she was battling two different forms of cancer. Angie came up with the idea of getting national attention to Leukemia and Thyroid cancer in hopes that a cure would be found. Through her persistence and perseverance, Jenny got worldwide attention, appearing in magazines with Boyz to Men, the Backstreet Boys, and Nsync. Stars such as Whitney Houston and Aretha Franklin were acknowledging her at concerts. Jonathon Taylor Thomas and Cleveland Browns quarterback Bernie Kosar became personal friends, calling her on a regular basis. Jenny's biggest supporter was President Bill Clinton. Jenny met President Clinton three times; I was with her on one occasion. President Clinton kept in touch with Jenny throughout his entire time in office; every time he came to Cleveland he called and wrote her letters. Jenny was on the front page of newspapers and TV reporters did stories on her. Hulk Hogan invited Jenny to his wrestling match when he was in Cleveland. When she met him back stage, Angie asked Hulk Hogan if he would help with the Leukemia telethon. Hulk Hogan said yes and the story was in newspapers and TV all over the world. Hulk Hogan became the main star for the National Leukemia Telethon and did nationally televised commercials on behalf of Jenny for the telethon. Angie and Jenny personally raised thousands of dollars for the telethon and were recognized by the Leukemia Society for all their work. Today because of new medical treatments for Leukemia and Thyroid cancer, doctors are optimistic that Jenny has been cured of both cancers.

Steve Piskor, President Clinton, Angie (Piskor), Jenny Moore, and Stephanie Moore

Chicago Gypsies circa 1960, Shanko standing in center, among the musicians are: Albert Duna, Davy Ballog, Tibor Horvath, John Ziga, and Bill Yedla

Chicago Gypsies

CHICAGO

Early records show a few Gypsies in Chicago in the 1930's. In 1936 the Chicago WPA orchestra had a five-piece Gypsy band. Chicago was the second largest city in the country. In the early 1920s, gangsters would make Chicago the talk of the world. Al Capone arrived in Chicago in 1919 and throughout the 1920s Capone's reign of terror would leave many mob members dead. 1926 reached the highest level of the mob war and the St. Valentine's Day Massacre was in 1929. In 1931 when Al Capone gained full control of organized crime, he was indicted on tax evasion charges and sent to prison in 1932. The mob war slowed throughout the 1930s with Capone going to prison, but it didn't stop. Frank Nitty was leaving prison when Capone was going to prison, and took over Capone's place. In 1943 Frank Nitty was indicted and committed suicide rather than go back to prison.

In the 1920's the Gypsies were frequently called to Chicago to play. Chicago has some of the finest restaurants in the county, and the Gypsies played in them. Al Capone lived a flamboyant life style and wanted only the best. The Gypsies played for Al Capone on several occasions and frequently for Frank Nitty. Elliot Ness moved to Cleveland, Ohio, in the

The Al D'Lacy (Shanko on bass) band

The Angel Sanchez Latin Band
On piano, Don D'Andre and my father, Julius Piskor on bass.

1930s and became Director of Public Safety, he ran unsuccessfully for Mayor of Cleveland in 1947. Throughout the years, the Gypsies of Cleveland often played for Elliot Ness. He died in 1957 and his ashes are buried in Cleveland's Lakeview cemetery.

By 1940, the Gypsies started to move to Chicago from Cleveland, Braddock and Youngstown and all the other communities. Chicago would become the largest settlement of Hungarian Gypsies. Louis (Kalo) Margitza and his orchestra played in the Blue Danube and Bela Babai and his orchestra played in Palmers Hungarian restaurant. By 1950, with the popularity of Xavier Cugat and Desi Arnaz from the "I Love Lucy" show, Latin bands were popping up all over the country, and the Gypsies were no different. With their ability to play any music, Gypsies were forming Latin bands, with two bands becoming famous and three musicians playing with famous bands.

From Chicago, the Al D'Lacy orchestra consisted of Joe Marconi, Tony Marconi, Albert Duna and Ray Richko. In 1952 they performed the song "Brazil" on the Georgia Drake TV show from Chicago and they became the orchestra for the weekly show. The leader of the band was Alex Lacy, Al D'Lacy's real name, the Gypsies called him "Shanko". Shanko was well loved and respected by all the Gypsies. If these Gypsies would have had a "King of the Gypsies", it would have been Shanko. Al D'Lacy and his orchestra performed for many years in Chicago, many movie stars went where they were playing, and Shanko became very well known.

Al D' Lacy (Shanko)

Elizabeth Horvath (Lizzy) Funeral, Chicago 1972

John Ziga (ya-low-low)

Gypsy kids help carry the bass at a Chicago funeral
Funeral of Albert Duna, 1967. Photograph property of the author

Chicago funeral

Chicago funeral 1952.
Photographs are the property of the author

There were many other Latin bands made up of Gypsies, in 1950 in Cleveland, the only Gypsy Latin band to play authentic Latin music was the "Angel Sanchez Quintet". The band consisted of Angel Sanchez (who was married to a Gypsy), Julius Piskor on bass (my father), and Don De Andre on piano, later Ernie Horvath on piano, and two Latin friends. The orchestra caught the attention of such Latin greats as Tito Puente, George Shearing, Willie Colon, Norm Morales and many others who frequently sat in to play with them. They performed on the Mike Douglas show and were the house band for the Dick Blake weekly TV show. They were the favorite band for the Arthur Murray dance studio and played most of their Ballroom dance functions.

Other Gypsies who played with famous bands were: Bill Richko who lived in Florida and played with Noro Morales; his brother Louis Richko, who lived in Johnstown, Pennsylvania and played with Charlie Palmieri; Willie Bandy who lived in Cleveland and played with Carmen Cavalero and also Johnny Bandy from Chicago who played with the Chicago symphony.

In the early 1960s Nandor and his Gypsy orchestra played on Rudy Orisek's International Café television show. The band consisted of Albert Duna, Albert (Buba-usha) Horvath, and Albert (Stacks) Balough.

Rudy Horvath funeral 1950 Chicago

Chicago funeral 1959
Photographs are the property of the author

Chicago funeral

Chicago Gypsies rehearsing 1964

Photographs are the property of the author

Archie Duna, Albert Horvath and Billy Yedla. All of them were very fine musicians. Albert Duna was considered among the best Gypsy Primas. The show featured a cimbalom duet with two great cimbalom players, Albert Horvath and Billy Yedla.

Around the same time period, the Gypsies of Chicago held a "Gypsy Concert" where about fifty Chicago Gypsy musicians played. The master of ceremonies was Al (Shanko) Lacy. Hundreds of people attended and news media from TV and newspapers covered the event. They featured the song "Shalamon" written by cimbalom virtuoso Albert Horvath. Albert Horvath was raised in Cleveland. He began studying cimbalom with his great uncle, Louis (Bum) Ballog. He furthered his studies in New York, learning cimbalom in the style of a Romanian, such as cimbalom Icon Tony Iordache. Albert Horvath is considered among the best musicians and was well respected.

Albert Lacy was born in 1923 in Cleveland, Ohio. The Gypsies call him "Achoo." He started playing guitar at an early age. He eventually switched to bass and studied with Joseph Guafesta, who played first bass for the Chicago symphony. Achoo went on to play with Itztak Perlman, Mel Torme, the great Jazz violinist Eddie South, Joe Parnell, and Tex Benedict. Achoo is considered among the best Gypsy bass players.

From left: Johnny Bandy, Helen Loysie, Silly (bass) Stacks, Chickie, Gus Horvath, Louis Miko (bass), Smokey, Geemshoy, Louis Rigo, and Frank Richko

Arthur (couldbe) Ballog funeral.
Photo by the author

Albert Horvath and Billy Yedla
This picture was captured off the TV program, that's why it is not of the best quality; I thought it would be better to see the actual performance

Rudy and Kenneth Horvath

He performed with the Chicago, South Bend and Eveningston Federation Symphonies. Achoo made many recordings, Achoo passed away in May of 2012 at the age of 91. His son, Donald Lacy is also a famous musician in Chicago and his grandson, Donny Lacy, is considered one of the top Jazz drummers and he started playing drums when he was able to hold the sticks. They both made records and play in Chicago's finest clubs under the last name "Demarco.

There are many great Gypsy musicians from Chicago: Alan Cole wrote songs that became standards in the Gypsy community; Steve and Mary Godla, Mary sings in the Romany Language; Billy C; Danny Ziga and too many others to list them all. Many of the Chicago Gypsies played in the finest clubs in Chicago, such as Jilly's and Gibson's on Chicago's famous Rush Street. Many of the Gypsies of Chicago became politically involved and became Aldermen in Chicago. This was an elected position that represented one of the fifty districts of Chicago. Alex Lacy (Shanko) and Albert Lacy (Achoo) became deputy sheriff for Cook County of Chicago and also worked for the Musicians Union.

Some of the Gypsies were in movies, the most notable of them were: Rudy Gabor, Edward Ballog, William Zurko, and Billy Richko who were in the movie *Return to Me* starring David Duchovny and

Joseph Horvath funeral, Chicago, June 9, 1950

Joseph Horvath June 9, 1950
Photographs are the property of the author

Joseph Horvath Chicago 1950

Funeral for Blind Mike 1950 Chicago
Photographs are the property of the author

Minnie Driver, these men are credited in the movie as Italian singers.

Today there are still many Gypsies living in Chicago. While there are still many musicians among the Gypsies, most of them are playing jazz and popular music while only a few Gypsies are playing traditional Gypsy music and that is almost at its end. About twenty years ago, groups of Gypsies from Cleveland, Detroit and Chicago, started to move to Las Vegas. Today there is a large population of Hungarian Gypsies in Las Vegas. Most of the musicians are playing in the casinos. I went to Las Vegas about ten years ago and while we were gambling in Treasure Island, we could hear this great music, but couldn't see whom it was. We finally decided to stop giving the casino all of our money and put it in our pocket instead of the slot machine and go to see what was going on. It turned out to be relatives of ours, playing in one of the biggest casinos in Las Vegas.

There are hundreds of Hungarian Gypsies living in Las Vegas but there isn't any playing traditional Hungarian Gypsy music. While Las Vegas became a new city for the Gypsies, it also became the first city where they completely lost their heritage.

Bella Ballog (Bendy) funeral Chicago 1953

Louis Ballog (Lio) funeral Chicago 1964
Photographs are the property of the author

Gypsy funeral circa 1950

Andrew Ballog Gypsy Orchestra

NEW YORK

New York is one of the biggest cities in the world. Some of the best restaurants and nightclubs in the world are there. New York is noted for having the best in entertainment. Competition is tough and musicians come from all over the world to play there. Like Frank Sinatra sings in the song "New York, New York", "If you can make it there, you'll make it anywhere" is a true statement.

The Yorkville section of Manhattan Island is known as "Little Hungary". The area of 2nd and E.79th Street had eight Hungarian restaurants and three Hungarian churches. The area also had a large population of Slovaks and Germans. One of the largest Hungarian restaurants was Zimmerman's, located at 46th and Broadway; it had three floors of fine dining and often had three Gypsy bands playing. Other Hungarian restaurants were: the Charades on 2nd and East 79th, the Café Grinzing on East 79th, the House of Vienna on East 79th, Tokay's on 7th Avenue and many more throughout New York. Many of the finest restaurants and hotels also had Gypsy music, such as the Waldorf-Astoria.

Jansci Rigo and Clara Ward circa 1904

The Gypsies settled in New York around the same time as in all the other communities. Gypsies from all the other communities frequently traveled to New York to play. Throughout the years many famous Gypsy violinists and orchestras played in New York. In 1896 the Princess Clara Ward, who was the daughter of a Detroit millionaire, went to a restaurant in Paris with her husband who was the Prince of Hungary. The Gypsy violinist Rigo Jansci was playing in the restaurant and the Princess was so captivated with Jansci, they fell in love and began seeing each other secretly. While both were married to other people, the news of the relationship got out and became one of the biggest scandals of the 19th century.

In 1904 the Princess and Rigo Jansci were married, and soon became Hungary's most famous couple. They often needed police protection from the crowds of people who would gather around them when they went out in public. The Princess had an eye for men and left Rigo Jansci for her third husband, and then left her third husband for her fourth husband. Jansci Rigo went to New York where he played with the New York Gypsies until his death in 1927. Over two hundred Gypsies attended his funeral; Zsiga Bela led the Gypsy orchestra. Rigo, who led a wealthy life with the Princess, died broke. A famous Hungarian

Zimmerman's in New York, circa 1940s
Zsiga Bela played here for years; he also played with Paul Whiteman and Erno Rapee
He died on stage at Zimmerman's in 1951

Gus Piskor Gypsy Orchestra
New York Gypsy Orchestras had a cimbalom player and a piano player.

pastry was named after him and is still a favorite pastry today. A few years after Rigo's death, his third wife died penniless and singer/comedian Sofie Tucker paid for the funeral.

Zsiga Bela was considered among the best cimbalom players in the world. He was born in 1890 in New York and his parents were from Kassa, Hungary. In 1910 he toured the country, then settled in Boston and finally moved back to New York. Zsiga Bela headlined in vaudeville, played at Radio City Music Hall and played in New York's biggest Hungarian restaurant, Zimmerman's, for many years. Many Gypsy musicians went to Zsiga Bela to further their studies in music, including my grandfather Louis (Bum) Ballog and Gusty Horvath. My grandfather on my father's side was Gus Piskor, who was also a cimbalom player. He and Zsiga Bela were close friends. When my parents were married in 1950, my father took my mother to meet his father, who lived in New York. That evening my grandfather took my parents to the restaurant where he was playing and in walked Zsiga Bela. Zsiga Bela knew both of my grandfathers and when my grandfather Gus Piskor introduced my mother as the daughter of Louis (Bum) Ballog, Zsiga Bela raised his finger to signify a number one and then said "he was the best cimbalom player, my equal" then Zsiga Bela sat in and played for my mother and father. Zsiga Bela died in 1951 and hundreds of Gypsies attended his funeral. The orchestra was led by Maxie Fransko and dozens of Gypsy musicians played including my grandfather, Gus Piskor.

Maxie Fransko was born in 1912 and his family hailed from Buffalo, New York. He settled in New York City. Fransko came from a long line of great Gypsy musicians. With his natural ability to play violin, he quickly became one of the best Gypsy Primas. He furthered his skills and graduated from the Manhattan School of Music. He went on to become one of the most recognized Gypsy violinists in New York. He played at all New York's finest places, such as: Tokay's, the Chardas, the House of Vienna, the Café Grinzing, Chez-Vito, and Chez-Lucies. He made records and dignitaries from around the world would often show up where he was playing. Maxie served in World War II, in a special branch of the Army. He organized a ninety-eight-piece orchestra, acting as concertmaster and soloist. In 1945 Mayor La Guardia proclaimed a week of "Victory Loan Days" and called upon residents, business and civic

leaders to display national colors. It was a final drive for the sale of E-Bonds to raise money for the end of the war. One of the events was the Hungarian-American Evening. Over 6000 people attended the event on Times Square. Maxie Fransko directed the orchestra, which included a cimbalom solo by Zsiga Bela. Six girls in Hungarian costume danced and Karl Hatvray of the Chicago civic opera sang. Mayor La Guardia auctioned off the Brooklyn Bridge. The bridge was sold to the highest bidder, and the winner received a four-foot model of the bridge. I recently met Maxie Fransko's daughter in Detroit. She told me that her father and Issac Stern were friends. Stern invited Fransko to his apartment for coffee one day and said to Maxie "It took me years of studying and practice to learn what you inherited naturally." Maxie Fransko died in Detroit in 1968.

Bela Babai was born in a Gypsy area outside of Kaposvar, Hungary, in 1914. A child prodigy on the violin, by the age of twelve there were newspaper articles about him playing at a café in Hungary. He arrived in the United States in the 1930s and lived in Chicago. He played at the Blue Danube, Ray Caruso's, and the Palmer House. In 1953 he moved to New York and played at the Chardas and the Esquire Room at the Waldorf-Astoria. Bela Babai's wife is related to the Detroit Gypsies. His piano player was Louis Horvath (Gypsies called him "Benjo"), his bass player was Oliver Horvath, and his cimbalom player was Billy Yedla, all from Braddock, Pennsylvania. They made many records with him. Bela Babai came to many affairs Gypsies had and I met him at a Detroit wedding twenty years ago. Bela Babai died in 1997

Zsiga Bela on cimbalom and Maxie Fransko
At Zimmerman's Restaurant

Racz Laczi Gypsy Orchestra

In 1931 the most famous of the Gypsy violinists arrived in New York. Racz Laczi, his wife Julia, his daughter Barbara (sixteen), his son Laczi (ten), and his eight-member orchestra were forced to wait six days in Ellis Island then had to appeal a decision to send them back. He finally won the right to enter the United States after having to post a $6,000 bond; the U.S. immigration said they feared the Gypsies would not want to go

back. Racz Laczi was considered the "King of the Gypsy Violinists" throughout the world. In Hungary he only played in the first class restaurants. He was the son of a Countess and Paul Racz. He was the favorite Gypsy violinist of King Edward, the Czar Nicholas and the Kaiser Willhelm. With jazz taking over the world, the Gypsies were losing the war on jazz. The old Gypsy musicians refused to change the music and Racz Laczi began working in second and third class restaurants, which was disgraceful for a man with his reputation. Newspaper articles were saying that the King of the Gypsy Violinists had been dethroned. There is not much written about Racz Laczi, I know he toured the United States, he was in Chicago and in Cleveland where the Gypsies of Cleveland met him. He went back to Europe and became an Icon of the Gypsy musicians; every Gypsy musician for over 70 years has paid tribute to him. There are violin competitions in his name and music conservatories are named after him. Symphonies and musicians worldwide have recognized his music. Years after his death, the Gypsies in Budapest made a video tribute to him and held a mock funeral for him, all the best musicians were there, led by Boros Lajos.

Boros Lajos eighteen years old

Gypsy musicians from different communities play for a funeral

Alex Lacy funeral 1942

The largest documented Gypsy funeral was February 25, 1930 in Budapest. The funeral was for the famous Gypsy violinist, Bela Radics, favorite Gypsy player of the Empress Elizabeth of Austria. Bela Radics' two daughters were married to Imre Magyari and Buda Sandor. It was announced that five hundred Gypsy musicians would play for the funeral. There were seventy policemen scheduled to keep order and once they learned of how many people were expected, they added three hundred police. Over 150,000 people turned out to see the five hundred Gypsy musicians play. It turned to chaos, people were stampeded and musician's instruments were broken from people trying to get so close. Thirty-four people were injured there. A few months later, Bela Radics' popularity was so great they decided to hold a concert in his honor.

Bela Radics Gypsy Orchestra

From the left: Spadga, Carl Bandy, Deon Ballog, Louis Miko, Frank Richko, Albert Ballog, Albert Horvath, George (Feki) Miko, Kalman Ginna, and John Bandy

Old Hungarian Slovak Gypsy Orchestra, circa 1900

This time it was held in the Great Stadium of Budapest. Over 200,000 showed up to hear 800 violins, twenty-six cimbaloms, eighty contrabasses, 140 violas and 124 clarinets. Bela Radics' headstone is a life-size statue of him holding is violin.

In 1956 the Hungarian revolution was going on and thousands of Hungarians fled Hungary and came to the United States. The U.S. labeled them as displaced persons or better known as DP's. Many of them went to Cleveland, Detroit, Chicago and New York. Some of them were fine Gypsy violinists and musicians. Kalman Banyak and cimbalom player Elmer Horvath played in New York's finest Hungarian restaurants. Throughout the years there were many European Gypsy orchestras that traveled to New York.

There were many Hungarian Gypsies in New York throughout the years and my grandfather and my uncle lived there most of their lives. There was little contact with the Gypsies of New York and the other communities. Some of the relatives that moved there were never heard from and some only kept in contact on a need to know basis. My great grandmother moved from Cleveland to the New Jersey side of New York and died there in the 1940s. Today in New York there are still Hungarian Gypsies living there, among them is a Doctor and a Lawyer and no Gypsy Musicians.

These Gypsies have been in this country for over 120 years. They brought to this country a tradition that was hundreds of years old when they were born. In an article in 1928, my grandfather talks about his father and grandfather being Gypsy musicians, he said, "They played cimbalom, as I do now." His grandfather was my great-great-grandfather. That would document around two hundred years of Gypsy musicians, two hundred years of ancestry and it documents generations of cimbalom players. In a newspaper article in 1930, Geza Duna said, "My father came to Cleveland nearly forty years ago and we still earn a living by playing the violin, like our ancestors did in Hungary for centuries."

GIPSY CHILDREN KEEP RACE'S MUSIC ALIVE

By MARION RUBENSTEIN

This is a story of a people the whole world can understand.

They have wandered thru many lands, yet where they go they are welcome, for everyone understands the message they bring thru their violins.

In Cleveland a colony of about 200 live on Columbus road. They are not ordinary gipsies, but "tzigans," Louis Balogh, who lives at 1955 Columbus road and who plays the cymbal in the Hungarian Gipsy Orchestra, explains.

"My people do not tell fortunes, they do not live by their wits, but they have earned their food and shelter for centuries with their music," Balogh said.

"My grandfather, my father before me—they all played the cymbal and I do now, and see even my little 7-year-old Albert, he can also play.

"See the little children out there on the sidewalk, they do not have to be taught how to play; it is as natural to them as eating," Janos Brenkacs, whom the colony addresses as "veyda," or chief, explained, as he pointed to a group of black-eyed youngsters who were holding an impromtpu concert on the sidewalk.

While 13-year-old Julius Ziga, 1963 Columbus road, played a merry tune on his violin, 4-year-old Florence Balogh and 3-year-old Alma Tokar danced barefooted, as their grandmothers had danced in the Old World festivals that were celebrated at the time of the pressing of the grapes.

Sitting on the curbstone, the Royal Gipsy Band, composed of 14-year-old Albert Duna, leader, Louis Balogh, Alex Lacey, Albert Horvath and Andy Balogh, held a rehearsal, while the girls danced.

Article in the Cleveland Press, 1928 interview with my grandfather Louis (Bum) Ballog. The article shows the young Gypsy boys, Julius Ziga, Albert Duna, Albert Horvath and Andy Ballog all learning to play from Louis (Bum)Ballog

History records of Hungarian Gypsy musicians date back to the 1400's in Hungary. Gypsy musicians were and still are considered unique. They are associated with playing violin, cimbalom and Gypsy music. They have influenced the great composers: Mozart, Bach, Beethoven and List..; the greatest violinists in the world: Jascha Heifetz, Stearn, Perlman..; these "greats" all went among the Gypsies. There are thousands of musicians all around the country, and it was the Hungarian Gypsy musicians, playing in the finest restaurants in the major cities around the country that drew attention.

As I was writing this book, it became hard to realize and believe that this great Gypsy tradition and heritage was coming to an end in my lifetime.

The traditional music died along with the older Gypsies who died in the 1960's and 70's. As the older Hungarians died off, so did the need for the music and the tradition of learning then playing it. By the 1970's, Gypsies that were around fifty years old and older were saying, "You can't make money playing Gypsy music. There's no place to play it anymore. Gypsy music is dead." In over forty years there has not been one of these Hungarian Gypsies who have learned to play the cimbalom and today there is only one cimbalom player. None of these Gypsies have learned to play second violin, viola, cello, or Gypsy bass. There are only a few violinists and the youngest of them is in his late 40's. There are no Gypsy orchestras anymore.

Today Gypsies younger than fifty years old do not know the music or speak the language. At times throughout the years there were so many Gypsy orchestras that we could not count them all. Today at a funeral, two or three musicians might play a few Gypsy dirges but for the most part, the younger Gypsy musicians bring electric pianos, guitars, drums and microphones and play American music. It's been over twenty years since a Hungarian Slovak Gypsy funeral has been in the newspaper. Today the musicians are all fine musicians and still play in all the best places, but none of them play traditional Gypsy music. They all play jazz, popular music and standards. The unique traditional Gypsy musician is gone and they are now mainstream jazz musicians.

Over the past forty years, not one child has been given the chance to learn traditional Gypsy music or play a traditional Gypsy instrument. There have been no Hungarian/Slovak Gypsies in America for the past forty years that have leaned any Hungarian Gypsy music.

With the talent in the bloodline, we can only imagine what great Primas or cimbalom players we're missing, and what great Gypsy orchestras we'll never hear. What's sad is they have the talent and ability to play the traditional Gypsy music, even if they learn it to play only among their own, and then go out and play whatever type of music you want to make a living with. Early Gypsy musicians played all types of music; today they only play one.

In the 1980's the Gypsies started to move further apart rather than living next door to each like they did for hundreds of years, today most Gypsies don't even know where the other ones live, and they prefer it this way. There is much dissension and a total disregard for respect among the Hungarian/Slovak Gypsies today. In only a few years Hungarian Gypsy music that was once the heart of these Gypsies will be gone forever. Today most of the young Gypsies are not even learning a musical instrument. There were Gypsies that held important positions and had the opportunity to do something to help these Gypsies keep their heritage and they did nothing. With the social networks today such as Facebook Gypsies are, for the first time, seeing pictures of their ancestors. With the genealogy research networks, some Gypsies think they can just put a name with a name and have a heritage. Names on a piece of paper are meaningless without a history and you should at the very least; know the history of the Hungarian Gypsies in the United States first. One that picks and chooses who is Gypsy, part Gypsy or discriminates against different types of Gypsies is the one to beware of for they lack respect and think they are better than everyone else. Who is to blame for the loss of such a great heritage? All of us, for listening to others that don't know, for not even trying, for giving up, for competing with each other to be better than the other in everything.

Today there is no interest in continuing the heritage and it will soon be just a memory.

Gypsies in Cleveland have broken an over one-hundred-year tradition by burying their seventy- and eighty-year-old parents in different cemeteries. The traditional Cleveland cemetery is Calvary Cemetery on Miles Avenue. Most of the Gypsies that did this were Gypsies that never lived the Gypsy life. Why do this to Gypsies that did live the life? No respect for their tradition. Artists such as Roby Lakatos and Kalman Balogh have taken traditional Gypsy music to a new level, modernizing it and incorporating it with jazz and fusion and they have become two of the most popular Gypsy musicians in the world. In my opinion, if our ancestors had known that the result of coming to America and the resulting effect of assimilation would be the loss of our heritage and Gypsy music, they would have never come.

In Europe the traditions still continue.

This book was written with the intention of preserving this great documented history of the Hungarian/Slovak Gypsies that kept Gypsy music as an important part of their life and death for hundreds of years.

This is a definition of a Hungarian/Slovak Gypsy from the Gale Encyclopedia: "Slovak Gypsies, historically sedentary, immigrated to the United States during the late nineteenth and early twentieth centuries primarily from Saros and Zemplen Counties in eastern Slovakia. Speaking a dialect of Romani, the men arrived singly or in small groups, and their wives and children followed later. Defined by musical performances, some settled in New York City, where they played in saloons, hotels, and theaters. Others, including the WPA Gypsy orchestras, established settlements in western Pennsylvania; Youngstown and Cleveland, Ohio; Detroit; and Chicago, where they played for ethnic and general audiences and performed industrial labor. Most remained Roman Catholics."

This was taken from my first web site about Hungarian Slovak Gypsies in America well over ten years ago. In the 1970s I knew this was happening and there was no way to stop it. I want to end this with a question to all the Hungarian Slovak Gypsies in America, fifty years from now, what could someone write about the Hungarian Slovak Gypsies of today?

The End

Comments

The only constant we have in our music is change…. Gypsy music is not gone; it has evolved just like it has for thousands of years. As we grow so does our music as we add different flavors from the environments and people we experience.

Steven Godla

My papu Al Lacy (Shanko) helped all the Gypsies. He worked for the musicians union, and helped them in getting playing jobs. He was a great family man and a role model to everyone. He truly was the "King of the Gypsies".

Jill Polo

Our people are one of the only nationalities still discriminated against. There are organizations for every culture except ours. If nothing is done to restore our culture it will be lost. We need a grant like any other culture to preserve our language and music before it is lost for good. We need to unite and see if there is a grant to preserve our culture like others have.

Delores Ziga

Our Culture is gone, we don't speak the language and everyone lives far apart. What I would like to know is why our people were so disliked. Our language is one of the oldest and comes from the ancient Sanskrit language of India.

Valarie Ballog

Gypsies are not a cult, religion or a practice. You have to be born from a Gypsy to be a Gypsy. Other people who practice traveling or Wiccan are not Gypsies.

Lawrence R. Horvath Jr.

It is truly a shame that traditional Gypsy music is almost gone among our Roma. In Las Vegas if my father and I don't go to play for a wedding or funeral, there is no Gypsy music played. I am only twenty five years old, and as long as I am alive, there will be Gypsy music played. It's a shame that the older Roma musicians don't teach the children how to play the traditional Gypsy music that our ancestors played for hundreds of years, and will live on forever.

Spencer Godla, Primas

We've been around and persecuted, as well as loved for centuries. I think there's little danger of the culture going the way of the Atlanteans, especially now in the Digital Age when music, photos and ideas can be shared instantly and globally.

Danny Hallup

Throughout history we were portrayed in many guises, some not so flattering. Yet we have also been admired for our lust for life! It has often come through in our music. It is hard to maintain our heritage in this modern world of technology. The close- knit family of old is now spread out globally.

Daniel Hallup

It breaks my heart to know that the gypsy heritage and music is slowly disappearing. Growing up, I remember going to funerals, weddings etc., and hear and see the Roma traditions and enjoying them. Knowing that my children and other gypsy children will not experience what I have, breaks my heart. They will not hear the music that I love and the traditions I've seen. We really need to bring it back before it's gone forever!

Tabatha Piskor Vanni

As a music educator and expert on the history of our Roma People and Their Music. I would like to state that it is a fact that our ancestors created the folk music in many parts of Europe. This is certainly true when you look at the history of the Hungarian Austrian Empire. At that time the folk music of Hungary was being created by certain Roma musical families.

Bill Duna

This book is a documented history of these Hungarian-Slovak Gypsies. It is a representative of all the Gypsies from this group. Some of the featured Gypsies in the book are the ones that were most documented. This is not intended to be a list of names.

Gypsies

Me and Roby Lakatos

Me and Deki Lakatos

Me and Bireli Lagrene

Acknowledgments

The Cleveland Press Collection
The Cleveland Public Library
Cleveland State University
The Western Reserve Historic Society
The Cuyahoga County Archives
Cuyahoga County Library Fairview
The *Pittsburgh Post-Gazette*
The Cleveland Catholic Diocese
The Pittsburgh Catholic Diocese
The Braddock Library
The Henry Ford Museum
The Collections of the Henry Ford
Elaine Horvath
George Batyi
William Ballog
Debbie Garber
John and Linda Ziga
Dolly Ballog
Alex Udvary
Tony Slepsky
James and Linda Ziga
Rose Piskor Zimecki
Dorothy Bright
Shelley Goodell Simpson
Professor Steve Balkin, Walt Mahovlich

Gypsy Violins

31869908R00151

Made in the USA
San Bernardino, CA
08 April 2019